A Life Worth Living

MY STORY

BILL YORK

A Life Worth Living
My Story
ISBN 978-0-9916124-5-1
Copyright © 2015 Bill York
P. O. Box 174
Catoosa, OK 74015
www.awsomecarz.com

Dedication

I want to dedicate this book to my mother. She always set a good example of living beyond what we expected of her. She would work tirelessly at caring for her family's needs, stretching meager amounts of food to completely satisfy us. She knew how to cook anything and make it taste good. She would work long hours with flour sack cloth to make dresses for my sisters and shirts for me. I believe she did all she could do unselfishly, spending long hours cleaning our house and clothes.

My mother did field work, milking, and other farm duties — even when she was pregnant — and some of the duties should have been done by someone else. She would always take her food last at mealtime so others would get exactly what they wanted. She left us no room for doubt as to whether we were loved. She loved everybody as instructed by the God she loved and served.

Contents

Acknowledgments 6

CHAPTER 1: Grandpa's Farm 9

CHAPTER 2: Big Adjustments 47

CHAPTER 3: Young Entrepreneur 81

CHAPTER 4: A Desire for More Than Enough 91

CHAPTER 5: From Labor to Management................ 109

CHAPTER 6: Family and Fun 131

CHAPTER 7: Excellence and Loyalty Pay Off............. 151

CHAPTER 8: The Challenges of Doing Business 167

CHAPTER 9: Land and a Beautiful Home 191

CHAPTER 10: A Hobby for the Family 227

CHAPTER 11: Seeing the World 257

CHAPTER 12: Our Spiritual Life 291

Epilogue:.. 310

Appendix A: Article I 311

Appendix B: Article II 315

Appendix C: Article III 320

Acknowledgments

My wife June was a constant help and encouragement throughout the development of the book. My daughter Lisa helped me in the early stages of writing this book. And my sister, Treva Kallman, helped scrutinize much of this book content. Debby Boyd was very helpful and a strong supporter of this endeavor.

I thank all of my friends and family who allowed me to share the events of my life that included them. Betty Cullum allowed me to write about all of the work-related and social activities that occurred between our two families. My brother, Steve York, had a lot of content written about him. One of my best friends, Jerry Lepper, provided the title of this book.

My good friend, Dick Belt, owns the blue whale, and Linda Hobbs is the manager of this attraction. I appreciate their encouragement and help in getting pictures of the cars at the whale site. David Norwood and Phil Wilson did most of the pictures. It's amazing what Phil is able to do with photographs. I'm grateful for their help.

CHAPTER 1

Grandpa's Farm

The 1940's were very special to me. The fourth day in this decade was the first day of my life, January 4, 1940. Not much of the three years that followed remains in my memory, but in my fourth year or thereabouts, I can remember some conversations. World War II was going on, and my mother and father were trying to get my father into an armed forces draft classification that would allow him to serve our country at home. We moved to a small town nearby, where he went to work at an ammunition manufacturing plant. They thought he would be more valuable to the United States of America as a producer of critically needed goods and services rather than as a soldier. Another strategy to get the deferment was working in a dairy, milking cows. America needed milk.

At four years of age I was very much aware of and concerned about the distressed position of my family.

Unfortunately, their best efforts to get Dad's draft classification changed did not work. Our government needed him more as a soldier than as a supply worker. He was drafted and sent to California to prepare to be a foot soldier for his country. So Mom, my sister, and I went to California to be near him while he was in training. As soon as his training was over and he was sent to Europe, we headed back to Oklahoma.

My dad was promoted to the rank of sergeant, and when my younger brother asked him how he got the promotion, he said, "I was the only one in my squad who was not killed." However, after he was a sergeant, I know of at least one event that made him a hero. Some soldiers are recognized for acts of bravery, but some are not. They may have been brave way beyond what was expected, but they never told anyone of these acts. I believe my dad was one of these. One day he told me that he had fought in the Battle of the Bulge. This was a very bloody battle in what is now the Netherlands. The opposing armies were dug in on both sides, and no progress was being made.

The German army had assembled a very large combat unit just across from where my dad and his squad were located. They started focusing firepower on a small area of the American battle line, which forced the Americans to retreat because they could not withstand the assault of this much larger group. When the retreat was called, everyone left his assigned position except Dad. He noticed two mortar tubes with large amounts of ammunition rounds stacked in triangles next to each tube. His thought was, *If I leave this ammunition here, they will be using it on us.*

Dad decided to feed all rounds into the tubes, which were pointed toward the pursuing army. He did not change any of the settings but simply fed all the rounds into the tubes as fast as he could. Of course, the tubes bounced around, as one round after another fired. This movement made the kill area fairly large. He said the attacking group must have been concentrated exactly where the rounds fell, because later he went through the area and found an unbelievable number of dead there.

My dad's superiors received medals for this act, even though they didn't know how it came about. They had left long before it happened. My dad was not recognized simply because he chose not to tell anybody what really happened. I guess he could have been too busy fighting a war. I wonder how many others were not commended for their acts of bravery.

These times during the war were also difficult for Mom. Though I was young, I was very conscious of the load she carried. My parents owned a home about twenty miles away from my mother's parents' farm. My grandpa was a very compassionate and giving person. He would help anyone who was not able to help themselves. At that time, there were a lot of people in need and no government services like we have today, so he provided housing and food for several people. Some of these people were physically disabled or mentally challenged. Some were family members, immediate and extended. Some were friends, and some were strangers.

My Grandpa Young

I believe that Grandpa went without food and housing at a young age, and this situation planted an attitude in him to help any needy person. I believe that this behavior on his part brought him many blessings from our Almighty God. I think he gave with a cheerful heart, and it left him feeling gratified. I also do not remember his benevolent behavior causing any problems in his family.

When Dad left for Europe, Mom chose to stay at Grandpa's most of the time. We would drive to our home about once a week. Sometimes, we would stay one night at home, then go back to Grandpa's for several nights. This traveling back and forth required a lot of gasoline, which was rationed. The government issued ration stamps sparingly to families, so Grandpa would share his stamps with Mom, allowing us to travel as needed.

Sugar, tires, and women's nylons, as well as a few other things, were also rationed. Sometimes we had the money needed to buy items, but they could not be purchased without these stamps. I can remember riding a lot of miles on the metal tire rims. And just in case you don't know, driving on the rims destroys them. They would get smaller and wider until the car would get so close to the road surface that it became impossible to continue driving on them. At times, we would ride on two rims and two tires. I don't think the tires manufactured during this period of time were very durable either, especially on those rough roads. They sure didn't last very long. We had a 1934 Ford we called Lizzie that had to be worked on frequently, and we pushed it often to start it. Lizzie was our only mode of transportation.

Everyone who lived at Grandpa's house had duties. These jobs consisted of caring for the farm animals. He had cows, hogs, chickens, guineas, and horses. They all had to be fed and watered, and the cows had to be milked. We had to gather the eggs. The milk and eggs were sold for income to support the needs of the people who lived there. My job was to feed the chickens and gather the eggs. The food for these animals was raised on his 160-acre farm. His prairie hay meadow was cut and baled for food for his cows and horses. He had about 80 acres of tillable cropland. On this land, he raised corn, wheat, oats, and a head-type feed. He had grain bins for each type of food. And, of course, he had a large vegetable garden.

Grandpa fed field corn to all of his animals. The corn had to be gathered by hand in the shuck and hauled and stored in the corncrib. When feeding corn, it had to be shucked and shelled. The shelling machine was hand powered. One ear at a time was placed into the machine. The corn was fed into the top receiver of the shelling machine and a handle had to be turned to remove the kernels from the corncob. The corn was fed to the cows, horses, hogs, guineas, and chickens. For the hogs, we would put the corn kernels into buckets of dishwater to soak and swell, softening the kernels. The hogs loved it, as these buckets would also contain table scraps. To feed the chickens, the corn required only shelling. Corn was only 25 percent of their diet. The cows and horses ate small amounts of shelled corn. Their primary diet was the grasses.

This is the machine used to plant small grain crops.

Other small grain crops were raised to meet Grandpa's needs. These small grains were planted with a machine called a drill. It placed the seed in rows about six inches apart, and the individual seeds were separated by about three inches. When the fields are full of standing grain, flowing and waving in the wind, they are absolutely beautiful.

These grain fields are full of rabbits and numerous other small animals. The small animals flourish in these thickly planted fields. They make these fields their home while they raise their families. The growing grain provides perfect cover for prey animals. When we harvested the grain, we removed the animals' cover and could see the baby rabbits. We enjoyed catching them and playing with them. After we played with them for a while, we would take them back to their home and release them.

Drilled crops complete their growth in late spring or early summer. The standing grain is cut with a sickle-type mower attached to and part of a machine called a binder. This cutter worked a lot like a pair of scissors. The binder, pulled by large draft horses, had a steel power wheel with cleats on it, which was in contact with the ground. Friction between the wheel and the ground allowed us to cut the stems close to the ground. The mowed grain was not allowed to fall and to lie on the ground while drying. The machine arranged the grain into ten-pound, loosely bound bundles and tied them. The heads of grain remained attached to the stems.

The total length of the heads plus stems was about twelve to fifteen inches. By turning the stems down and standing the bundles up with the heads on top, you could keep the wheat or oat heads from spoiling while waiting for threshing. The bundles were placed in cone-shaped piles, which were called shocks. The shocked grain stood in the heat of the day, with the summer winds flowing through the loosely tied bundles. This was nature's drier. This drying process was a very important part of harvesting, because any dampness would cause mold.

The grain was left in the field several weeks to thoroughly dry. The purpose of this fifteen-bundle shocking step was to help the threshing crew to gather fifteen bundles at a time with only one stop. By placing the bundles down, leaning in toward the middle of the shocks, they became very stable and could resist strong wind gusts. Most farmers raised both wheat and oats and harvested them in the same way.

These small grains were separated from the stems with a machine called a thresher. The threshing job was mostly a bartering type of activity. They made sure that no one was shortchanged. Men of the community and family members arrived on the selected day to help with the threshing job. It was usually a one-day event on these small farms. Most of the farmers only raised enough grain to feed their own animals. Nothing was sold and no money changed hands, except the man who owned the thresher would charge a nominal fee.

Everybody was involved in the labor. Men, women, boys, and girls had a responsibility. While the men were doing their jobs, the ladies were busy preparing one of the best lunches you could possibly eat. My job was riding a horse around to give the crew drinking water. I was five years old at this time.

A day before threshing, a smaller crew would arrive

to move the large thresher onto the chosen location. Usually it was centrally located in the field. The machine had to be set up properly. The thresher was powered by a stationary tractor, using a long, flat belt that ran from the power wheel on this tractor to the thresher. This belt had to be aligned and tightened correctly. All this was done before the threshing began.

A threshing crew in action.

The threshing crew consisted of about a dozen men. Some of the men would bring their own teams of horses and wagons to the grain field. These men had two different kinds of wagons. One type was equipped with a well-made box, built to haul the harvested grain to the storage bin. The other type had a large flat bed with a tall headboard used to convey the bundles to the threshing machine. The tall headboard and large flat bed enabled the men to stack large numbers of bundles on each load. The tool used by the men loading and unloading the bundles was the pitchfork.

These loads of grain were carried to a two-man crew, who stayed at the thresher. This crew's job was to slowly feed the bundles into the thresher. The thresher put out straw on one end and clean grain came out a screw conveyor on the side of it. Usually there were four or five of the wagons collecting bundles. Only two wagons were needed to haul the processed grain. When the job was finally completed, the grain was inside the landowner's grainery and the straw would be in a large straw stack. Just as soon as your threshing job was completed on your farm, you were preparing to go to the next farm to help those who had worked on yours.

Head feed was raised and used only for animal food. It grew on a stalk about three feet high. The heads were bushy with small grains about the size of a BB and usually contained about one hundred grains per head. It was cut off the stalk by hand with a knife. These heads were stored in a bin, similar to the wheat and oats bins, until needed. It was fed to the chickens while still on the heads. The chickens would peck the granules off one by one. When it was fed to other animals, it was usually ground up in a very fibrous meal. The farmers relied on this feed to provide protein for their animals, some of which were work animals.

During the years that I was young, the American farmer was in a transition period. They were changing from farming with horses to farming with tractors. Some of them made this change as soon as they could. Others changed when they thought they must. A farmer with the aid of a tractor could produce several times as much as a farmer using horses. During the years I was involved as a child, some jobs were still being done in the old-fashioned, slow way. This was how it was done on Grandpa's farm during this period of time.

Horse-drawn sickle mower.

Personally, I think I was blessed to be a witness of this transition period. Sometimes I'm sure farmers had a tractor sitting at the house while they were using their horses to do the work because they may not have had the tractor implements to do the jobs they needed done. Grandpa's hay meadow was cut with a horse-drawn sickle mower. The hay had to lie in the hot sun about four hours to cure or dry, and he checked it frequently to be sure that it would be dry enough to store without molding. The way he checked it was to take a small portion, hold it by the two ends, and pull on it while rotating it about with one hand to see if it would sheer or come apart. If, by pulling on it and applying this twisting action, he was able to pull the sample apart, it was deemed cured and dry enough to bale. He was careful to check it frequently, because the quality was affected if it lay in the sun too long. It would dry out too much. Once he determined that curing was just right, he was ready to proceed to the next step.

This buck rake was used to place the mowed hay in rows.

At this point he would arrange it into rows with a buck rake. The buck rake had two wheels, one on each end with about twenty circular spring steel teeth. These

teeth were about 24 inches in diameter and were a little over a half of a circle. The area where the circular
teeth were open allowed the grass to enter into the rake
mouth, filling the area with a tightly packed collection
of hay.

The rake was set so the teeth were touching the
ground. The hay was cut so all grass fell the same direction. The raking was done across or perpendicular to
the lay of the grass. When the curved teeth came into
contact with grass stems then it was pulled over more
mown hay until the quantity would build up and the
rake became full. At this point the teeth were raised,
leaving a row of collected grass the width of the rake.
This was repeated until a line of rows was established
across the entire field.

A proficient rake operator could trip the rake at the
right time to align the next load of collected grass with
the previously placed loads. The raking and tripping
process was repeated until the field was completely full
of cured hay in rows. These rows were then scooped
up with an implement called a go-devil. The go-devil

had eight, foot-long, wooden fingers which were brass-tipped. They were about eight inches apart. The fingers were attached firmly to a headache rack, which would hold the hay as these fingers slid along the ground under the windrows. The grass would pile up on top of these long fingers and against the headache rack. When the operator decided the go-devil was full, he took the grass to the baler. At this time he let the go-devil down and backed up. This operation enabled the grass to slide off the fingers next to the inlet of the baler.

Men were present at the baler to hand feed hay into it with pitchforks. This was repeated throughout the day. The baler was powered by a gasoline engine. A hard-working, well-organized crew could bale three or four tons of hay per day. I was fortunate to get to see some old diehards bale with a horse walking in a circle to power the baler. Their production was much lower than the gasoline-powered machine. Regardless of how it was done, the end result was that the farmer had hay in the barn to feed his animals through the winter.

All farm people are caretakers of their animals. They

see that they are well fed and have clean water available for them. The large animals were supplied water from the farm pond. The hogs' water came from a well. This well was a small hole in the ground, about twenty-five feet deep. It had a hand-operated, pitcher-style pump, which had to be primed. To do this, you had to pour in some water to prime the pump. The leather gasket had to be wet in order to make a seal inside the pump, so it would pull a vacuum in the pipe going down to the water in the well. The handle of the pump had to be worked up and down to get the water flowing into the water trough. It took a lot of effort to work the handle until the needed quantity of water was received.

For household water, we had a hand-dug well about four feet in diameter that was located about twenty feet from the house. This well had a rope with a pulley and bucket to bring the needed water to the surface.

Feeding families and friends was a little bit different than the way it's done today. People who lived during these years were healthy and trim. The food was fresh and had no preservatives. We had no snack food to tempt us. Dining was looked forward to because we were tired from the work we had to do and needed more energy. I'll never forget all of us sitting around Grandpa and Grandma's long dining room table, located in the dining room next to the kitchen. This table had benches along the sides and chairs on each end. We were fed family-style, as everyone was back then.

The meat came from the farm animals and, occasionally, wild game would fill our plates. The vegetables came either fresh from the garden or canned from the garden. We ate three meals per day, with almost no snacking between meals. Grandma always had large quantities of bread made from scratch. We either had biscuits or corn bread with each meal. She would set the leftover bread on top of the wood-burning stove. If anyone ever asked for food between meals, she would give them one of those leftover biscuits or cornbread, which would be very dry and hard from the heat. This was good strategy on her part. After you had one of these snacks, you seldom wanted to snack between meals again. Other benefits from her system were that the heat kept the flies from the leftover bread, and with so few people snacking on it, the hogs got more bread.

I'll never forget the delicious fried chicken, fried pork side meat, and ham. Beans and soups were often served and were also very good. All these foods were cooked on a wood stove. We made our own butter, and buttermilk and fresh whole milk were common items on Grandma's table. Back in the forties mealtime was very special. One reason, as I said earlier, was that everyone was hungry from working hard and no eating between meals. Another reason was that the ladies were dedicated to preparing food items clean and right. They even made their own butter molds, just to enhance the table.

One of my friends told me that he once brought a friend home with him to have dinner. During dinnertime his friend got a biscuit and cut one corner off of the molded butter to butter his biscuit. After he had eaten that biscuit he proceeded to get another biscuit and cut another corner off of the beautifully molded stick. When he started to do this the third time, my friend's grandma could not take the butter butchering any longer. She spoke up and said, "It looks like you could at least cut all your butter off of the same end."

His friend replied, "I don't see what difference it makes, Grandma. I plan to eat the whole thing." This shows just how much pride women took in their food preparation.

I think Grandpa's goal was to be as self-sufficient as possible year round. He and Grandma had a large vegetable garden and a good-sized orchard. This allowed them to have an abundance of fresh vegetables and fruit. Our family group did all of the tilling, hoeing, and fruit and vegetable picking. We were all involved in the canning of these items too, which was very labor intensive. The growing season started early in the year and lasted until fall. Canning required most of us to contribute a measure of hard labor to make it successful. Once the abundance of garden and orchard products was harvested, we had to think about how we could best preserve them for consumption through the coming seasons.

Potatoes needed to be stored in a cool, dark, dry place, and then they would last most of the year. To preserve fruit and vegetables beyond their shelf life, they needed to be canned. To do the canning requires you to pick, clean, peel, slice, and pack them into containers, then heat the containers to temperatures that purify and accomplish vacuum packing. Fruit can also be dried for later consumption.

We canned green beans, carrots, tomatoes, pickles, beets, corn, peas, cabbage, okra, squash, beans, and sauerkraut. Of the fruit, the canning included peaches, pears, plums, and apples. Later I realized how much variety in food items our Creator provided for us, and we used every bit of it. Grandma's pantry was usually full in the fall and almost empty in the spring. Living back then was much different than the way we live today.

Grandpa's farm had a natural gas well on it. He checked it out to see how much it would produce. He wanted to be sure it would produce enough gas to meet his needs. After he was convinced it would, he purchased fifteen hundred feet of pipe, plumbed it to his house, and bought gas stoves to heat the house and garage. The garage did not have doors on it, so he simply placed a gas stove in front of his old pickup truck and lit it. This stove burned all winter, keeping the truck warm and ready to go anytime he wanted to use it. He also plumbed the house for gaslights. They really lit up the house. They were great in the wintertime, but in the summertime these lights produced too much heat, so we simply did not light them.

In the summertime, with no gas being used, the gas well filled with water and would not produce any gas the following winter. Grandpa called an oil well service company and had the water bailed out. As soon as the water was removed, here came the gas again. His solution to the water problem was, as soon as the wintertime use ended, he simply lit a torch in the edge of the orchard near the yard. The torch provided us with a yard light. At night the bugs came to the light of this torch and tried to fly through the flame, which resulted in them falling to the ground injured, so the torch served as an insect control device. The orchard torch got rid of fruit damaging insects and fed the chickens the next morning.

A young boy may have a good bit of chores and work to do on a farm, but he will find time to do his share of playing. When I was four and five years old, I played there often. The children would chase each other or throw sticks for the dogs to retrieve. We would play with marbles, balls, and build toys with wooden spools and boards. The games that we played were the same ones other farm children all over this part of rural America played.

Grandpa had an old battery-powered radio. No matter how carefully he managed the radio time, it consumed the power, which frequently required battery replacement. We would cannibalize the old batteries to get the carbon sticks, which we used to do our artwork. As children, our canvas was frequently rocks, boards, or hard clay earth. Remember, this was pre-electricity years for farm people who lived in remote areas.

This fine example of the Victorian style is beautiful to me.

Grandpa and Grandma's house was located near a small town and was the same style as those we lived in during the early years of my life. Some people are buying these Victorian-style homes and fixing them up today. There are a lot of differences in the size and quality of these homes. I took pictures of small and simple and large and complex to show how they can differ. The houses in these pictures are the finest examples of the Victorian style I could find. It's beautiful to me.

When we were playing in the yard, next to the county road, we would see or hear anyone coming down the road. All artist work or other playing activities ceased until our curiosity was satisfied. We wanted to know who was passing by so we could report it to our elders. I guess we were the first road reporters. Travelers didn't come by often. Some were in automobiles, others were on a horse or in a horse-drawn wagon, and occasionally someone came by on an old tractor. Those who passed by in vehicles daily were the mailman and the iceman. When the iceman came we ran to greet him. He would often give us a small piece of ice, which would thrill us. The iceman was delivering ice to most farms, where the ice was placed into an icebox that kept our food and milk from spoiling.

This house is the same style that we lived in during my early years.

I think our group of small children could have a good time playing with almost anything or with absolutely nothing. At the end of a busy day, in a dark house, we always got ready for bed early. The beds were crowded. People were lying at the foot of the bed as well as at the head of the bed and slept very close together. I was very energetic at this age and did not want to go to bed. So mostly I got into the bed last or near last. My only choice was either at the foot of the bed or on the very edge. If I moved much, I fell off the bed. That happened many times. It seemed that a lot of time passed while I was falling, but the floor was always there to catch me. Falling off the bed is a rough way to be awakened!

The mattresses were straw ticks. Do you remember that in thresher activity, straw was collected on one end of the machine? This straw was used to fill the heavy cloth mattress covering, resulting in a comfortable mattress. You could lie in one spot and wiggle a little bit, and the movement would make a depression that perfectly fit your body. The straw acted a whole lot like memory foam.

With no fans or air-conditioning, the summer heat would force us to put our beds outside in the yard. Being outside in the summer months, coupled with going to bed as soon as it got dark, caused kids who were not sleepy to lay on our backs and look at the stars. I thought celestial bodies that I saw streaking across the sky were falling stars. I was sure we would soon run out of them, because there were so many falling each night.

When I look back as an adult, it surprises me how much uneducated people knew about star constellations. They could find and identify several by their names. On the nights that we slept outside, if Grandpa detected any lightning or thunder, he would wake us up and tell us to grab our bedding and go to the cellar. Most of the time none of the storms materialized in our area. It was an interruption in our night's sleep, but we were soon back in bed and sound asleep. I honestly don't remember any insects keeping us awake or bothering us while sleeping outside. By morning everyone was rested and ready to face another day.

For farm families to have a good breakfast during the winter months, particularly bacon, you had to prepare well ahead of time. The first step was breeding the sow at the proper time, in order to have a litter of pigs on the ground early in the year. Grandpa wanted four weaned pigs about the first of April. He would feed them plenty of corn and table scraps to make them the right size for the fall butchering. I remember he had us put a few small lumps of coal into the hog pen, so they would eat it and the coal would worm them. I don't remember him having any problems keeping his feeder hogs healthy. He wanted the hogs to weigh about two hundred and fifty to three hundred pounds at butchering time.

Grandpa's sons and sons-in-law butchering crew

When the weather started to cool off in the fall, each farmer usually asked for outside help to come to his house on a certain day to help do the butchering. Grandpa's help consisted of his son and two sons-in-law. Preparation began early in the day, before the helpers arrived. He had a cast iron container filled with water, under which he placed a gas fire. The heating took about thirty minutes to bring it to a boil. Each hog would require a pot of scalding hot water. They took a fifty-five gallon drum and laid it on its side with the closed end partially buried in the ground so it would hold the hot water. They bailed the water from the heating pot to the treatment barrel.

The first thing the helpers did was to kill the hog and allow it to bleed. This took place at the hog pen. Then the hog had to be transported to the scalding barrel. The next step was to get the hog into the barrel of hot water. The hog had to be turned around and scalded from the other end. If the hot water bath is done properly, the hair can be removed easily by scraping it with a knife. Then they would remove the entrails and other organs, as well as the head. Hog handling done like this, by hand, required strong men. The men had to be careful not to burn themselves with the hot water.

The next step was to cut the meat up into the desired sizes. Most of the pieces would weigh between ten and fifteen pounds. Grandpa had a smokehouse built above the cellar to smoke and store his meat. This building had many shelves along the walls and a center section full of shelving, with edge trim to facilitate salting and prevent the salt from falling to the floor. These storage compartments were about eighteen inches square with four-inch trim.

The salting process included a layer of salt in the bottom of each bin. They placed the cut of meat on top of a table and rubbed salt into the meat. Then the piece of meat was placed into the bin and submerged in salt. Each hog would provide about fifteen pieces of meat. The above-described steps were done on each hog until all the meat from the four hogs was in the storage bins. The liver meat had to be eaten fresh, because we had no refrigeration. We ate a lot of liver for a day or two!

The farm families also needed lard for cooking. The fat was removed from the inside of the hog, then cooked until the liquid lard was separated from solids. They mixed some of the lard with lye and heated it until lye soap emerged. The homemade lye soap was the only soap I remember us having during this period of time.

When taking a bath and using this lye soap, you had to keep your eyes closed very tightly until you were thoroughly rinsed off. If you ever got lye soap in your eyes, the painful experience would cause you to be sure it did not happen again. Another side benefit we kids liked on butchering day was that they removed some skin and made pork rinds. The pork rinds were a very tasty snack. They were only available for a couple of days, so snacking didn't become a habit.

In the mid-1940s, our government established co-operatives to enable the farm families to have electricity. Private utility companies did not want to build these systems, because the number of houses per mile of supply line was not sufficient to make it cost effective.

Therefore, the government decided to underwrite these projects. As a child I did not understand all of this, but as an adult, I now understand the role the government played in enabling us to have electricity. I realize how much more comfortable it made us.

Grandpa's entertainment included hunting just for fun. He would get into his pickup truck and invite us boys to accompany him to watch his dogs chase jackrabbits. The hay meadow was located on the south part of his farm. When we arrived, he would drive around the meadow slowly until a rabbit would get up in front of the truck, at which time one of the dogs would take up the chase. Grandpa would point out to us how the dogs cooperated with each other. The second dog waited for the first dog to turn the rabbit back toward the truck, and then he would take up the chase. A fresh dog in the chase sometimes resulted in a catch. Without their cooperating, they had no chance of catching the rabbit.

Grandpa was amazed at how smart his dogs were, and that they could once in a while catch a very fast jackrabbit by using the cooperation strategy. He always hunted by riding in his truck. He had severe asthma attacks and had a hard time just walking to the truck.

Another type of activity Grandpa invited us to participate in was picking up walnuts. He had a way of making anything we did fun. He would load us up in the truck and travel to a neighbor's farm, where they had walnut trees. Early in the fall of the year, the walnuts would fall off the trees in a green shell. The walnut shell or skin had a lot of oil in it. If you crushed this covering, placed a bunch into a burlap bag, then put the bag into a pool of water where fish were present, the oil would make the fish come to the top and lie there. You could simply pick them up! This procedure did not kill the fish, and if you didn't pick them up quickly, they would soon swim off. The fish were so small that I don't remember us ever getting a mess of fish to clean and eat. We were always looking for something good to eat. Nevertheless, we still did this a few times. The only real benefit was that it was fun for a child, and Grandpa enjoyed seeing us have fun. And this activity provided us with walnuts to enjoy for the fall and winter months.

Often Grandpa and Grandma's married children would arrive at the farm for visiting and good home cooking. Each family brought a dish or two for the meal. This was a very common event, and everyone looked forward to fun and dining. Grandpa ordered a general run of baby chickens, which means he bought approximately 50 percent roosters (male) and 50 percent pullets (female). The pullets were kept to replace the older laying hens. The roosters were kept mixed in with the pullets until they became frying size, then they were meat for the table. Most of these special meals were on Sundays.

During this time of the year we all looked forward to fried chicken, country gravy, and fresh vegetables from the garden. On the particular Sunday I'm remembering, my aunt baked a layered chocolate cake. They transported it up near the glass behind the backseat. When they arrived, they got out of the car and carried it into the house. They left the windows down on the car, and a chicken got in and made a deposit on the backseat. The color and texture of this deposit looked just like the cake icing. My cousin saw it, and thinking it was icing, he immediately picked it up on his finger and put it into his mouth. He soon came out of the car gagging and vomiting continuously for several minutes. At the time, nothing was funny about this event. We did not know why he was acting this way. We knew he was in trouble, but we didn't know why until he explained what happened. We have enjoyed reliving this event many times.

Sometimes traveling from our house to Grandpa's didn't work out like we expected. One time we were traveling in Lizzie when an automobile backed out of their driveway and hit our car dead center on the driver's side. The impact destroyed both doors on that side of the car. These cars had no airbags or seat belts. We were left with head to toe soreness and a badly damaged car. The person who hit us did nothing to reimburse us for the damage they did to our car.

As a young boy, I saw how much effort the adults

expended to get an acceptable performance from their automobiles. Most of these cars were produced in the 1930s, and some were produced in the 1920s or earlier. The manufacturers built transportation vehicles, which were going into the hands of people who had no idea how to operate or repair them. They were as likely to do something that hindered the performance as to do something that would help the vehicle perform well.

These years yielded a next-generation of cars that had many changes, most of which were not understood by the buyer. I believe that my seeing the automobile evolve developed a passion in me for these transitional years' vehicles. I'm sure that my favorite year was 1933. One of my friends, my family, and I put together a website in an attempt to show some of the cars of this era. See www.awsomecarz.com. In the back of this book, I have also included three articles I wrote about our country's history with the automobile. I hope you enjoy them.

CHAPTER 2

Big Adjustments

Like everybody else, we walked to and from school. I liked walking *from* school a lot better than I liked walking *to* school!

The first schoolhouse I attended was a one-room building with a large coal stove in the center. It had boys' and girls' cloakrooms to hang up our coats and shelves to set our lunches on. One wall faced away from the road and was mostly windows to provide us with light. On one end of the building was a small stage. There were about thirty student desks and one centrally located teacher's desk. Outside, it had a storm cellar and boys and girls' toilets.

For our playground, we had a set of four swings and a merry-go-round. We played tag, hide-and-seek, and baseball. We would also go to the top of the dirt mound that covered the cellar and play "king of the mountain." Recess and playground activity were the only part of school that agreed with me. When I started to school, I had not been exposed to any kind of restriction and could move about anywhere I wanted to, so sitting still in a classroom was difficult for me. I especially had a hard time adjusting to the stern, crusty, determined older lady who insisted I sit down and learn a lot of things that I, at five years old, had no interest in learning.

A few whacks across the back of my hands with a wooden ruler had me wetting my pants and looking at learning a little differently. In this lady's defense, she probably did not have the luxury of spending much time with any one student. She had about thirty students in eight different grades to teach. I may have needed to be a little more mature before starting to school.

At the end of my first grade, my life changed dramatically again. Dad came home from the war, and we moved from Grandpa's house back to our house. I moved out of a house full of people into a house with only my mother, my little sister, Dad, and me. During the day Dad was at work, and I don't have too many memories that were very interesting.

I became friends with a boy who lived down the street from me. His house was an old railroad hotel. It consisted of two buildings, had no water or electricity, and was just concrete walls, much like a prison. The buildings were two stories, with room for about twenty families in each, but only two families lived there. The parts they didn't live in were rundown, empty rooms.

We lived in this small community setting for about seven months, with a lot of days of nothing to do but play and go to school. One day Dad brought an old, 26-inch bicycle home. At six years of age it was way too big for me to ride in the normal manner. I soon learned I was able to ride it if I put my right leg through the opening under the bars that were between the seat and handlebars. With my leg through that opening and my body on that side of the bike, I had to lean the bike in the other direction in order to balance it. This made steering very difficult. When I needed to turn the wheel to the right, it was hard to turn, and when I needed to turn to the left to maintain balance, it wanted to turn by itself. When someone rides a bike in this manner, it sure looks peculiar, but this was the only way I could ride it. I soon grew a little taller, and by shifting my body to the left and right on each pedal stroke, I was able to ride in a normal, upright position. A mistake or an unexpected bump as I slid my body back and forth across the bars sometimes resulted in a very painful groin injury. Nevertheless, I rode the bike and enjoyed it.

This is a 1940, 20-inch bicycle. It is not like the 26-inch bicycle I learned to ride on, but it is of that era.

Our house had three rooms and no running water. There was a country store just across the train tracks.

We had chickens in the backyard and a well in the front yard. I don't believe Mom and Dad were happy with the house. They owned this place for only a short time and then decided to sell it and buy a larger one in a larger community. The decision to move is unclear, but it was probably related to Dad's potential employment opportunities. All I know was that it caused me to be uprooted and to leave another set of friends.

Moving from an almost rural area to the middle of a town changed my life. Traffic was passing within fifty feet of me no matter where I chose to play on the city lot. Everyone in my age group already had friends and activities that did not include me. It seemed like anyone I had contact with was a misfit or a bully. One of the boys who lived next door always wanted me to participate in rough physical activities, which usually ended up with us wrestling. He was a year older than I was and much bigger and stronger. I always lost and believe he enjoyed hurting me. I was tough and seldom hurt badly enough to surrender or cry, but I did not like to play with him.

I soon became friends with another boy who treated me well. At least, he didn't hurt me. His father worked at a garage downtown that we walked past on our way home from school. Each day my new friend would stop by the garage, and his father gave him money to purchase candy and ice cream. He was selfish and would not share anything with me. I sure did get to watch him eat a lot of treats as we traveled the rest of the way to my house.

One morning while walking to school I found a dime. I told the teacher about the find. One of the boys in the class said that he lost it, so the teacher made me give him half of it. I knew he didn't lose it, because it was out where the cars parked and not on the sidewalk. She made me share my wealth with him, but she did not make me like her decision!

I did not perform well in the second grade, and after consulting with my parents, it was decided that I would repeat it. They said I had started to school at too young of an age, and they thought I needed another year of maturity. I do not know if I did any better the second time around. Either I did better or they got tired of messing with me, because I was allowed to go to the third grade.

After two months of attending the third grade, we moved again. Dad wanted to be a farmer. He rented a farm in the same school district where I started to school in the first grade. This move to the farm began a long, arduous series of unpleasant changes in my life. I was nine years old.

Dad gave me the scary job of going after the newly purchased cows, and I knew that big, mean cows could hurt small boys. The other big obstacle I had to overcome was that the cows were in a very large pasture, the grass and weeds had grown all year and were very tall and thick, and there were lots of snakes in them. The pasture had a creek running through it, so I would push my way through the underbrush along its banks. At times I could see the grass and weeds moving in front of me. I did not know what was moving them, but I knew it was some kind of snake or four-legged critter. The ground cover was so thick that many times

I could not find the cows.

The first time I came back without the cows, Dad sent me to look for them again. When I didn't find them the second time, because it had become so late in the day, he took me back to show me how to find them. When he failed to find them, he bought a cow-bell and put it on one of the cows. The bell made it a little easier for me. At least I only had to make one trip.

Dad was rough on me but, in his defense, he was broke and had no tools to do his farming. Some of his struggle was vented on me. I believe in his eyes, I was his property to do with as he pleased. This kind of thinking was a carryover from an earlier generation. Therefore, I had a difficult time during the first years of being on the farm. Then I had some kind of fever and became very sick. I could not keep any food down and became so weak that I could not sit up. We had no money for a trip to the doctor. Mom and Dad simply hoped and prayed that I would get better.

Finally, after a couple of weeks, it became so bad that Mom asked me if I could think of anything that

I thought I could keep down. After thinking about it, I told her that maybe I could keep some orange pop down, and it worked! In a few minutes I started feeling the positive effects of the very badly needed nutrition from the orange pop. A six-pack got me back on my feet, although I was still very weak.

I had been sick and out of school so long that they took me back to school too soon. I remember at recess I walked out to the toilet, and when I finished doing my business, I squatted down by the wall on the sunny side and watched others play. As I sat in the sun, I was invigorated after only a few minutes because the Vitamin D in my body was being replenished. Looking back, it doesn't surprise me that I had gotten sick. We drank water out of an old cistern that had mosquito larvae in it.

On the farm, we raised a beautiful field of corn. I think the field was about forty acres. When the corn was ready to harvest, Dad kept my sister and me out of school to help him pick it. We had a 9N Ford tractor. To release the clutch on this tractor required a force in the vertical direction, so Dad had my seven-year-old sister stand on the clutch bar. Her weight was enough to disengage the clutch. She had to stand on a small bar while the tractor was sitting still, in gear, and running.

Dad's picking program consisted of him driving the tractor to the field with a trailer attached. The tractor and trailer would knock down two rows of corn, and my job was to pick the corn off of the stalks, shuck it, and throw it onto the trailer. Bending over all day long made my back hurt a lot. Dad's job was to pick the corn off the three adjacent rows next to the trailer, shuck it, and throw them onto the trailer. My little sister's job was to stand on the running board where the clutch lever was, hold onto the side of the steering wheel, and steer the tractor when it was in motion. She remained in the same position when told to stop, stepping upon the clutch bar until given the instruction to move again. The travel time was the only time she could give her feet a rest.

This cycle was repeated hundreds of times throughout each picking day. If we worked hard from morning to noon we would pick a trailer load. Then we would go to the barn, and Dad would park the trailer next to the corncrib. My sister and Dad would go to the house and eat while I unloaded the corn from the trailer into the crib. The unloading took about thirty minutes. I felt cheated to have to work even more, after doing the hardest job in the field, which was picking up the rows that were on the ground.

When I finished unloading, I was allowed to go to the house and eat a cold meal quickly. Then we were off to repeat the cycle. After corn picking quitting time, I went to get the cows for milking. It took us about two weeks to harvest the corn, then we attended school until cotton-picking time. This is how a poor sharecropper's children lived in the early 1950s.

Some of our personality traits are greatly influenced by the environment we are raised in. Dad had a very strong, unwavering attitude that he was correct and the rest of the family must yield to him. We all had to conform to his expectations, or he would react in a physical way. These events occurred suddenly, and most of them were very cruel. I never could figure out what would or would not set him off. It seems like the audience that was present may have been a big factor. As an adult I have concluded that it must have been more important to him to be the dominant person in every group than most people. I do not know what made him like this, but I know his behavior had a bigger impact on me than anyone else in the world.

The more severe events occurred when I had visiting friends. I probably acted different when I had friends present. Looking back, maybe some of the blame falls upon me. After I got older I realized that the only solution for me was to stay completely away from him, but it did not keep me from loving him. As a teenager I was hungry most of the time, because by not going home I wasn't able to eat with the family.

I do believe that people are like animals when it comes to establishing dominance. The world is comprised of bullies and those who have to deal with them. Bullies can be encountered anywhere: in school, at home, and next door. This home environment programmed me to be more tolerant of being pushed around elsewhere. I talk about this because, as a small boy, this was the only life I knew. I didn't like it, but I saw no way out of it.

Later in life I thought of leaving altogether, but I had a very loving, caring mother who saw my burden was heavy and tried to compensate for this problem. I would have endured anything to keep from hurting her. This was a life-long problem for her too, but she loved him as I did. He was her husband and my father. We were supposed to love him.

When I got older I visited my parents often. I was the oldest boy and the only son who lived near them. One day, when I had just completed a small business deal that placed five hundred dollars into my hand, I decided to go and see Mom and Dad. Spontaneously, I decided to share some of my recently acquired gain with them. I handed them each a one hundred dollar bill and instructed them to buy something nice for themselves. This act brought a statement from Dad that surprised me and left a memory I cherish. He stated that he just didn't understand it, but it seemed like I was able to make more money without even trying than he ever could make while trying as hard as he possibly could. This was one of only a few compliments that came from him. And what he did not understand was that my situation was really just God's blessings sent my way as I followed Him.

During the farming years, a number of farms were advertised for sale. We were struggling with the sharecropping style of farming. In these young years of my life, I listened to Mom and Dad talk about how they wished they had the money to buy a farm. I heard their wish over and over as different farms became available. I had sincere desires to help, but at the age of twelve had no means of doing anything. At this point, we were committed to continue to invest labor and money to make a crop. The toil of trying to be successful as sharecroppers continued for five long years. My younger sister heard the same conversations and felt the same way. When we both had become financially able, we helped our parents realize the dream of buying their own farm.

The family tried very hard to make the sharecropping work, but in the end we were not successful. Not being able to make his dream of being a successful farmer come about was very hard for Dad. His frustration was vented on our farm animals and me. One day, we were trying to get the cows into the barn, and they were not cooperating. He was frequently hurting them in various ways, which probably contributed to the animals not wanting to go into the barn. Sometimes we do things that render the opposite results we want.

I must have done something in my effort to help him that he didn't like, because he grabbed a one-by-four board and started hitting me with it. The board had a rusty, two-inch nail sticking out of it. He hit me three times before it stuck and was hard for him to pull out. The first two times it must have penetrated into soft tissue and came out easily. When he realized what was happening, he began apologizing for his actions.

Not keeping yourself under control frequently causes you grief. The event was not severely painful to me. When you are struck with something flat and heavy it just numbs the area where you are hit. However, on other occasions when he lost control of his temper and punished me, the pain was severe.

I believe that when you do things that do not conform to the teachings of Jesus Christ, like treating others with respect and kindness, you are subject to penalties. None of us are exempt from the consequences of our actions. Even though he was faithful to the church for many years, his dedication did not leave him unaccountable for his actions outside the church. I am grateful that he took us to church, because I learned about Jesus there. The Bible says that the Lord treats all of us the same. I know I also did some things that were not pleasing to Him and suffered for doing them. Some of the things I did may have been more unacceptable to God than what Dad did.

Sometimes what we do is planned, and other times our actions are not thought out beforehand. If an act is deliberately committed, knowing it is not acceptable to God, I believe we are placing ourselves in a worse position. We are all sinners and our failures and transgressions are only erased by Jesus' loving act of forgiveness. He loves us when we are not very loveable! When we stop depending on only ourselves and place ourselves in His care, we will not have an anxious heart. He lifts us up when we are down.

Dad rented a piece of agricultural land to farm, which was located about ten miles from where we lived. The field was in a river delta area. After a flooding rain, Dad wanted to know whether the floodwaters had done any damage to his corn crop. Dad, my uncle, and I went down to inspect the crop. In our travel to the field, we had to walk a long way down a closed section line. While we were walking, we came to a brand-new fence, built high enough to prevent large, grazing animals from jumping over it. As we progressed along the trail, we discovered that two horses were following along at a distance from us. They seemed like they did not trust us and wouldn't get too close. We were walking parallel to this new, beautifully built fence, when my uncle asked if we wanted to have some fun. Of course, our reply was affirmative.

He told us to continue to walk at the same pace and watch the trick he was going to play on the horses. He was wearing a leather jacket and went into the forest. The trees were on our left, and the fence was on our right. He stepped behind a large tree and pulled the bottom of the jacket up above his head, while leaving his arms still in the sleeves. The horses noticed that something was different and became cautious. When they reached the point where my uncle had stepped behind the tree, they started walking slowly to the tree with their ears pointed in his direction.

As soon as the horses were close, my uncle jumped out and started popping the jacket by moving his arms apart over and over. The horses bolted and ran toward the fence. When they reached it, they did not have time to turn. Their heads hit the wire, and they pushed the wire about ten feet before their back feet left the ground. They turned the prettiest somersault over the fence and were not hurt. Each landed on their feet and continued to run. My uncle said he had no idea that would happen. He said, "Don't tell a soul about this!"

So we never talked about it.

When we were farming this bottomland, at harvest time we were required to pick the corn and haul it to the storage bin located on the farm where we lived. It took a full day to pick, haul, and unload the corn. We pulled a two-wheel trailer and a four-wheel trailer to the field. After we had filled the two-wheel trailer with corn, we hooked the four-wheel trailer to the back of the two-wheel trailer and filled it with corn. When we finished picking, Dad told me to drive the tractor and trailers home.

When I arrived at the house, he met me and instructed me to back the four-wheel trailer beside the door of the corncrib and unload it. A four-wheel trailer is very difficult to back, because you have a swivel point on the drawbar and a rotating front axle. I not only had to contend with these challenges, but also I had a trailer between the tractor and the trailer I was instructed to park next to the crib. I think he stood around the corner and watched me struggle with the chore, and I'm sure he was surprised to see me accomplish it!

One Sunday we had company at our home. The sky turned very dark, then it began to rain heavily. I was standing at the window, looking out over the flat prairieland that was our yard, watching the rain pour. The yard looked like it was covered with standing water. Suddenly a bolt of lightning hit the house. The sound was deafening, much louder than a clap of thunder, and it scared everyone in the house. As soon as we determined that no one was injured, we began to assess the damage. The two gables located at each end of the house received heavy, splinter-type damage, and at the top of the gables the boards were completely gone. All the light bulbs were broken, and the screens on the windows had holes in them. The electrical wires also received a lot of damage.

We soon discovered that the floor in the kitchen had broken boards that were smoking. We pulled other boards out of the floor and saw flames. Dad ran outside and turned off the gas. He discovered that the bolt of lightning had burned a hole in the steel gas line. We put out the fire quickly, and I reported that, as I was looking out the window, I had seen three balls of fire hit the water in the yard. They sizzled and danced as they got smaller. Dad said, "You didn't see any balls of fire. That was just spots before your eyes because of the flash of lightning."

When the rain stopped, I went outside where I had seen the balls hit the ground and examined the area. I found burned grass in all of the three locations where the balls of fire danced. I immediately went inside and told Dad. What I did not realize was how unusual ball lightning was. I've never seen ball lightning since.

Even though we plowed, planted, weeded, and sprayed, we didn't have much cotton to harvest. The boll weevils ate it up. Only a few cotton bolls produced the snow-white product to sell. In a few days of picking, we completed the harvest. Some crops simply do not do well enough to justify the cost of growing them. We had borrowed money to make a crop, which didn't yield what we expected. Then we had an unhappy banker, who didn't get paid, and there was no money to plant a crop next year.

Your inability to get a satisfactory crop yield soon hinders your relationship with the landowner, and a disappointed landowner will eventually ask you to move. He will try to find another sharecropper who is more successful at farming. You have to find another landowner, who is willing to take a chance on you to continue farming. When you find the farm you will occupy next year, then moving begins. Almost always, these farms need much repair on fences and buildings, and since we had made no money, we had to do the repairs ourselves.

Having to make repairs with no material makes you think differently. You have to use available materials in a way that is not the usual way of using them. For instance, you might improvise by using willow sprouts lashed together to build your corrals, or you might tear down an old, dilapidated structure to get materials. If you had fencepost, wire, and wood, the repairs would be much easier and faster. If you don't, you simply do the best you can with what you have. Living this way causes you to think differently your entire life. I know this training enabled me to be more successful.

Our second farm was much like the first one. It had agricultural land surrounded by pastureland. The backside of the pasture was only about one-eighth of a mile from our house, but there was no way for the cows to get across the agricultural field. The cows had to be walked around this field, which was over a mile and a half to the barn. In the morning at milking time, they were usually in the pasture close to the house; but at afternoon milking time, they were almost always in the back pasture. I was the person who had to get them to the barn at the correct time. These trips were required in all kinds of weather.

I never thought much about the quantity of miles these trips added up to in a year's time, and I also walked to and from school. Dad continually complained about how hard I was on shoes, but neither of us considered how many more miles I was required to walk than he was. Even if I never played walking or running games — and not counting all the miles I walked chopping, picking, and doing other related chores — I still walked about eighteen hundred miles more than Dad did per year. As an adult, I'm not surprised that my shoes, exposed to all the weather-related conditions and an extra eighteen hundred miles per year, had a short life.

On a typical winter day as a twelve-year-old, I would be awakened by a shout from Dad, telling me to get up and go build a fire in the coal stove downstairs. It was always very dark, because it was four o'clock in the morning. One of those mornings, it had snowed overnight. I knew it had snowed, because the bed and floor were covered with a thin layer of snow. If I had remembered to bring in corncobs, coal, and kerosene the night before, it was much easier to build a fire.

We had no television or radio to get a weather forecast. We simply woke up and looked outside to see what we had to deal with each day. One evening I forgot to bring in the materials for the fire the next morning. During the night it rained, and a layer of ice coated everything about an inch thick. When I went outside, the sky was so dark, it was hard to find the coal pile. The ice was so thick, I had a hard time breaking through it to get to the coal. Finding coal that did not have ice and was dry was next to impossible.

It took me about forty-five minutes to get the fire started. It was so cold, I wasn't able to get warm before my next assignment. I had just gotten back in bed, when Dad told me to get up and get the cows for milking. It was slippery, and I slid down a long cow trail in the dark, trying to find the cows. When I located them, I brought them back to the barnyard to be milked. This chore took another hour to complete.

While Mom was milking the cows, I fed the chickens and hogs and put out hay for the cattle. When the first cows were milked, the milk was brought to the separator room, where I turned the crank handle on the separator to extract the cream. This cream was sold to a company to make ice cream. The money from the cream and eggs we sold was an important part of our income. We were barely able to buy groceries with this small amount of money.

Next I ate breakfast and got ready to walk one and

one quarter mile to school. None of this hardship hurt me permanently; it just made me tough, so I never gave up in difficult times later in life. As I said earlier, we sharecropped for five years, so this was my life during that time. The farm chores had to be done seven days a week in all kinds of weather. I think, during the five years, each year we did this chore routine about eighteen hundred times. About a quarter of those days were in the winter, requiring me to get up in the cold house and build a fire in the stove.

One of my childhood friends, Jimmy, read my first version of this book. When he gave it back to me, he said, "Bill, you wrote about all the hardships and bad times. Write about the good times too." I promise you that I left out the most unbearable treatment I received during these years. There was very little to write about that I would consider good times. We were viewed as the family with the least material wealth, and life was pretty much tough in all dimensions. In school, we never had money to spend on treats, magic shows, music shows, or plays held in the gymnasium. Our classmates noticed we were the poorest family. In and around church, they also knew we were on the lowest rung of the economic ladder. What we wore and the vehicle we drove were strong clues. Children are cruel when these circumstances exist, and our peers shunned us.

For a lighter moment and in an effort to satisfy my good friend on the subject of fun times, I will tell you about an occasion when I enjoyed playing a trick on my dog. This happened when I was about twelve years old. I had a mixed-breed dog that looked like a toy fox terrier. He was very loyal and obedient to me. This was sixty years ago, and I have had a lot of dogs throughout my life, so I actually do not remember his name. I'll call him Rags. He loved me, and I loved him.

Rags was always with me when I was outdoors. He loved to hunt anything. He was small, but he didn't know it! He was brave way beyond his size. He would defend his territory against anything, no matter how big the intruder was. If he could get behind a large dog and get hold of the bigger dog's rear leg, the fight was over. When he would finally turn the large dog loose, it immediately left our area. When he showed this kind of bravery, I showed my appreciation by petting him and telling him he was a good dog. He loved this kind of treatment and went looking for something else to run off our land. He loved attention, even if it was while I was playing tricks on him. I played tricks on him often.

One day while I was busy chopping cotton, I noticed that Rags had smelled a snake in the fencerow, next to the county road. When he smelled a snake, he exhibited a unique behavior pattern. He did not like snakes and smelled all the area around him, trying to locate it. The area consisted of about 50 percent last year's dead grass and 50 percent new growth green grass. The old grass was concentrated next to the ground and was very thick. This gave the snake the opportunity to be completely hidden.

As I watched Rags search, I decided to quietly move over next to him and slide the handle of my hoe under the dead grass on which he was standing. When I did this, he jumped straight up about four feet and began to run in midair! Then he came straight down, right where he did not want to be. He repeated the same rou-tine, running in place in the air, with the same results. He did this two more times before he was successful at getting far enough away from the "snake," allowing him to run on the ground instead of in the air. This event was so funny, and I've enjoyed the memory over and over for years. Rags did not hold grudges either! He immediately forgave me and went on hunting as I continued to chop the cotton. It was a comfort to know he was protecting me against other snakes while I was moving around.

We lived on this second farm for three years. These were the most miserable years of my life. I suffered more during these three years than any other period of my life. Nevertheless, the hard conditions made me tough and determined to be an overcomer.

One year, Dad planted a very large quantity of cot-ton. My little sister and I started chopping this crop when the stems of the plants were the size of the stem on a wooden matchstick and had two leafs. We chopped every day except Sunday through the hot summer.

When we finally finished chopping cotton, the plants were so big that it was easier to bend over and pull up the unwanted plants than to try to cut them.

I felt so sorry for my sister. She was only nine years old. Her arms were not much bigger than the hoe handle she was using. To help her as much as I could, I would finish my row and turn around and help her finish her row. As small as she was, she did an excellent job chopping. When it got late in the day, she would be so tired that she could hardly continue working. One day, Mom gave my sister a watch and instructed her on what time to quit working. Mom told her that we were to come to the house when the big hand got on eight. Later, when I asked my sister what time it was, she replied, "It's five minutes until ten minutes past six thirty." That reply made me think hard in order to figure out what time it was! We have laughed about this many times since.

Dad and Mom took us to church several times a week. Dad always tried to give a dollar when the collection plate was passed, and Mom agreed with this practice. Everyone in the church congregation had more income than my family had. We always arrived at church about thirty minutes early, because my dad played guitar in the service and had to set up his amplifier. It was a common practice for the children of the church members who came early to walk to the ice cream store and have ice cream before service began. What goes on in this world is not always fair. The preacher was a part-time preacher, but the church paid him a small salary. So I'm sure the ice cream for his children was purchased with money that dad had given as an offering from our family. My little sister and I simply walked with them and watched them eat their ice cream.

We ate pretty good at home. On some mornings I was able to bring in a wild, cottontail rabbit for our table. I caught these rabbits in box-type traps, which I built. They were in the skillet and cooking without even getting cold. A breakfast of fresh, fried rabbit, eggs, and country gravy is hard to beat on a cold winter morning.

One of those difficult fall days, Mom ordered me

six, brand-new, white T-shirts. I never had any new clothes and was so proud of these shirts that I wouldn't cover them up with my old, tattered jacket. The teacher at school continued to tell me to wear a coat when it was well into the winter! At this time I was thirteen years of age.

You would think that things could not get any worse, but they did. I realize I have only mentioned my younger sister, but by the time I was thirteen there were five kids in our family and Mom was pregnant again. This new baby made six. Dad could not walk without crutches, because he had a pinched nerve in his back. He could not use his right leg at all, so the crop we harvested that fall was mostly my responsibility. I was feeding the farm animals and milking eleven cows night and morning. My forearms got so tired milking, I had to rest them frequently. It was important to stay with each cow until I got all its milk; otherwise, the cows would go dry, and we would not have the income from the sale of the milk. The milking caused my fore-arms to build up so much muscle, that I looked like

Popeye, the cartoon character, when he ate his spinach! When the daily chores were completed, I had to go to the field and see that the small quantity of cotton was picked, weighed, and loaded into the truck. Then Mom drove the truck to the cotton gin and sold it.

While this was going on, Dad was not doing well and eventually had to have back surgery to relieve a compressed nerve. The doctors fused three vertebrae, which gave him mobility again. The recovery took about six months, at which time he could do light work.

One disappointment after another doomed our family's farming career. To be successful, you have to have a savvy leader. I don't believe my Dad ever told a lie after he gave his heart to the Lord. Since *he* didn't tell lies, he assumed nobody else did. He believed everything he was told to be truthful.

We worked all year to raise our calves to be large enough to sell. Then a cow buyer would come by and tell Dad that our calves were worth less than they were really worth. He would lie to Dad and buy them cheap, then sell them at a much higher price. The buyer probably reaped much of what our family should have received, and he only owned the calves a few hours. Even as an adolescent, I could see we were shortchanged. When you are obligated to give the landowner large percentages of the gain from the farming, there is no room for mistakes. Another element that was against us was in the early fifties northeastern Oklahoma had droughts, which sent many farmers back to town for work.

The farm workload was lighter the last year because Dad surrendered and gave up on his dream of being a farmer. What made it less demanding on us was that we didn't have to put up winter feed for our animals. Late in the fall we had a farm sale and sold all of the farm equipment and livestock. We only kept our furniture, clothes, and pickup truck. Then we moved back to town.

CHAPTER 3

Young Entrepreneur

By the time I was a teenager and we moved back to town, I had been making enough money to cover almost all of my clothing needs and was fairly independent. I started to think about how I could earn my own money and looked for miscellaneous jobs to meet other needs. Some of the jobs I found were far enough away that I needed transportation. I had an old Cushman motor scooter that needed some work to make it roadworthy, so I saved my earnings until I had enough to fix it.

My dad told me he knew a very good mechanic, who would overhaul the engine. All I had to do was remove it and bring it to him, along with thirty-five dollars. I asked Dad to take the engine and money to the mechanic and to relay a message to him: I wanted a strong engine. Only when it was returned to me and I installed it did I realize how successful he was at making it very strong. I had a ride that pleased me. In fact, I was able to outrun the new Cushman Eagles.

The scooter was both reliable transportation and a great pleasure ride. Through the first year of warm weather, a friend and I would ride our scooters down the ditches along the highway and pick up pop bottles on weekdays, when I was not working other jobs. We would sell the bottles for two cents each and take our earnings to purchase gasoline fuel for our scooters, as well as Pepsi-cola drinks and one-fourth pound Baby Ruth candy bars for a good, healthy lunch.

These Mustang scooters are the type I wished for in the 1950s.
Now I have four.

One day when we were hunting for pop bottles, I found a twenty-dollar bill. I went home and told my mom about my good fortune. She was happy that I was blessed with the find and suggested that I send ten dollars to a special missionary we knew. He was spreading the Good News of Jesus Christ our Redeemer in Mexico. She also suggested that I could spend the remaining ten dollars on school clothes. I listened to her and complied with both of her recommendations. I believe that any economic support a person contributes to a servant of the Lord puts them in a position to receive some of the credit for the success of that person's godly work.

Late in the fall of that year, I approached my uncle about letting me bring his tractor to town and plow gardens. He accepted my offer and terms, and I started my plowing business. After word got around that I was doing a good job for a fair price, I had plenty of gardens to plow in my spare time. I was to give one-half of the money to my uncle after we bought the fuel. When the plowing was over, I had enough money to purchase an automobile that was only five years old. My uncle had an equal amount of money.

This success created an entrepreneurial attitude in my mind. I did anything that earned me an income during my high school years. Most people who saw me laboring at these various jobs, especially my class-mates, were not impressed. They even suggested in the class prophecies that fifty years from then I would still be mowing lawns. You do not know how that makes a young man feel when he already is struggling with low self-esteem. Later in life I acquired a lot of distressed rental property. I often thought of the class prophecies while I was fixing, cleaning, and especially mowing over-grown lawns. However, my classmates failed to see that I would *own* all the property I would be working on!

Shortly after I accumulated a nice savings from the plowing and mowing work, I started thinking about getting a car. Of course, Dad knew about my inten-tions. One day he came home and told me that he knew where I could get a very good 1951 Ford with a brand-new engine. I had enough money to cover the owner's asking price. I trusted his judgment and handed over my money to Dad for the purchase. He drove it home after he completed his day of work. When I saw it, I was tremendously disappointed. It was a faded, green color, and the seats were dirty and tattered. The seller had chewed tobacco and spit on the floor on the passenger side of the car. However, mechanically the car seemed to be in good condition. As disappointed as I was with what I had purchased, I made it look the best I could. I cleaned it up, polished it, and soon was able to purchase new floor mats and seat covers.

I enjoyed dating and driving all over the countryside. On my first date, a group of upperclassmen talked about drag racing. I certainly was not going to allow them to think I was afraid to race them, so I accepted the challenge and we were off to a desolate stretch of road just outside of town. My car had a six-cylinder engine, and I had had hundreds of hours of experience driving farm equipment. I knew how to get the absolute most out of a vehicle, whether it was a car or a tractor.

When we got to the racing location, one of the five

boys in the other car got out to flag us off at the starting line. He counted off the designated numbers and dropped his arm, at which time the race ensued. There was no race to it; I simply outran him. When the race was over, he flashed his headlights. I supposed this was a signal for me to stop. As the driver pulled up beside me, he informed me we were going to race again. He said he spun his tires and could not get traction. He didn't intend to, but he did a beautiful burnout.

As the flagman readied himself again, the driver shouted for everyone in his car to get out. Still, the outcome of the second race found him way behind again. This time I just kept driving. I remember thinking, *Maybe this six-cylinder engine is not so bad after all.*

I still did not like riding around in an unsatisfactory looking car. My mind labored over what I could do to change it from the ugly looking brute it was. I decided to make it into what we now call a lead sled. I shaved the nose and decked it. That means I took all the factory chrome off of both ends and smoothed the chrome locations. I added fender skirts, lowered it on all four corners, and added some unique chrome. Once I had the look that I liked, I started thinking about color and preparing the surface for paint. I located a generous man who wanted to help me after he finished his work in a body shop. We painted my car Siesta Gold evenings and nights in a shop behind his home.

The paint job included seventeen coats of hand-rubbed, lacquer paint. I wanted to stop sanding when the primed surface looked perfect to me, but the painter kept telling me to sand it more. When I had the surface acceptable to him, he started a series of steps I didn't understand. Most people do not know about the quantity of work that is required when applying a show-quality paint job.

He sprayed a light coat of the finish color paint all over the outside surface three times. There wasn't much color, and it still looked ugly. He then told me to return the next day for sanding. I returned and sanded long and hard until he suggested I quit and let him apply another series of three coats of paint. When he finished this time, I could see more of what I wanted to see. His instructions were, "See you tomorrow for more sanding."

Each time we sanded, the grit on the sandpaper got finer and finer. When we repeated this the third, fourth, and fifth time, I wondered if his motive was a paint job or punishment! I had never imagined painting a car involved this many steps. Also, when you sand a beautiful car with sandpaper and make it dull, it looks awful. It's difficult to continue doing this over and over. Ultimately, he let me quit sanding and he stopped painting, and I was pleased when it was completed.

The sheet metal looked perfectly straight. The paint looked like you were seeing deeply into it. I don't remember seeing another paint job as perfect as this one. Now all I needed was a new upholstery job, and soon I had the money to pay for it. When that was installed, I had a completely new-looking car. I sure did like my finished ride, and the girls liked it too. I drove this car until I graduated from high school.

This car is not the body style of my first car,
but the paint job looks similar.

The most rewarding job I had, and the easiest, was driving a school bus when I was a senior in high school. When I got this job, I picked up the other high school students first. I addressed the older group before the younger students got on the bus. I told this group that they were just as old as I was, and we could have a pleasant ride home if they would help me keep order on the bus. I reminded them I would be busy driving the bus in a safe manner, and I appreciated their helping me out. I believe they took pride in the responsibility I shared with them. They had a pleasant ride home and always arrived safely. Sometimes simply communicating with people totally changes the outcome of situations we encounter in our lives. That was another valuable thing I learned in all my endeavors to earn money during high school.

CHAPTER 4

A Desire for More Than Enough

When I graduated from high school, I weighed 156 pounds and was six foot, four inches tall. Anyone who knew me then was looking at a very hungry young man! My attitude was to neglect my body and take care of everything else. I also acquired a tobacco habit. The expenses of operating an automobile and buying cigarettes took all of my money. Dad gave me two dollars one time, but he could not afford to finance me or my activities. My five younger siblings had basic needs requiring his earnings.

My solution to constant hunger was smoking, which reduces your appetite. When I got hungry, I didn't eat. I simply smoked another cigarette. Of course, smoking did not conform to my parents' teaching or their rules. Lack of good food and smoking were hard on my body. The addiction was my fault and a very bad decision. I learned a lot about what I didn't want to do by doing it! However, not eating was not totally my fault.

After graduation I worked as a plumber's helper for a short period of time while waiting to do my military duty. Soon the waiting time passed, and I was off to basic training at Fort Leonard Wood, Missouri. They issued me clothing and boots. When I put the fatigues on, you could not tell there were any legs in those loosely fitting pants, but they began feeding me three regular meals each day. With the food and exercise, I started gaining weight. We wore the fatigues through training, so they were washed in hot water frequently. This made them shrink, and rigorous training increased my muscle mass. You could soon tell there were legs in those pants! Before the six months was over, I had difficulty getting the pants on.

This change in my body size was something new to me. Now tall and muscular, I was often selected to face opponents in simulated combat training. In hand-to-hand combat training, the cadre would select the most imposing men to defend themselves at their assigned stations in the training course. Then all the remaining soldiers were directed to fight the selected soldiers one-on-one at these stations. This exposed me to hundreds of opponents while training in hand-to-hand combat.

The men running through this course were instructed to attack by using preplanned moves selected by the trainers. I soon learned that many men would not follow the rules. Some combatants were determined to get the best of the selected station opponents. After being caught off guard a couple of times, I was much more cautious. If a course trainee did anything indicating he was not going to do the assigned move, most of the time he would find himself lying on the ground. In real combat, I'm sure the enemy would not do what you expect. I'm of the opinion that the devious fighters made the planned training much better than it would have been had everyone followed the rules.

This new role of being the one feared didn't change my feeling of dislike for anyone taking advantage of others. I remained a compassionate, caring person. I would not have liked myself if I had allowed this change in my size to interfere with who I wanted to be. I think it takes a big man to forgive and let it go rather than getting mad and getting into fights.

My training started in Fort Leonard Wood, Missouri, and ended in Fort Ord, California. In my second eight weeks of advanced training, they put me into a group of soldiers who were destined to go to paratrooper jump school. This type of conditioning did not include walking anywhere. We *ran* everywhere we went! The army's specialized training classes sometimes were twenty or thirty miles from the barracks. At times they had trucks to come out to these training areas to pick us up and haul us back, but the officers would tell the drivers we wanted to march back to the barracks.

One night the cooks had to keep dinner hot until

about eleven o'clock. This march was a very long one. After a long day of training and all that forced marching, most of the group were too tired to eat. Not me! I ate every chance I got. I guess I was a chowhound. Many men who went into the army say that the chow was not good. Let me go on record as saying that the army had very good cooks and good fresh food, except when we were required to eat C-rations. Some of the cans containing these C-rations were dated and apparently about fourteen years old.

Some of our training was conducted up in the mountains on Hunter Leggett Game Preserve in California. This was such an unusual climate. At night the temperature would get down to near zero degrees, but during the day it would rise to about one hundred degrees. We started the day heavily dressed, and as the weather warmed up, we took off clothing until noon. Shortly after noon, we had to start putting on clothing. This trained us to cope with wide temperature swings.

Each soldier carried one-half a tent as part of his backpack. We were issued three wool blankets and a wool sleeping bag. The cadre assigned me to a man with whom I was to share a tent. He and I elected to put two blankets on the ground and placed the sleeping bags on top of the two blankets. This left us with four more blankets to put on top of us. The first night we left our clothes on when we went to bed. That night we got very cold. Before the stay was over, we were wearing all the clothing we had, including six pairs of socks.

We soon found a source for purchasing a candle about the size of the large end of a baseball bat. This candle burned throughout the night, providing some warmth even though it was risky for fire. We still got cold, but we did not have frostbite. Keeping warm became a problem for all soldiers, including our instructors. In fact, it became critical to do something to avoid permanent injuries. Those in charge decided to have warming tents delivered and set up in our camp. It helped us, but there was not room for all of us to sleep in the warming tents, so we were not allowed to do anything except warm up and go back to our own tents. As you would expect, we soon needed to go get warm again. It was tough, but we survived the cold un-scathed.

One day we were advised that we were going on a 24-hour march that would include running war skirmishes. We were supplied with one canteen of water and C-rations. Our rations contained water purification tablets along with the food. I drank my water much too soon and was getting extremely thirsty, but I knew that the Santa Lucia Mountains were pristine with lots of snow streams. It was dark when we came to a small one, which allowed us to step over it.

When the line of men moved along and it was my time to jump across, I stooped over and put my canteen under the water to let it fill. About the time it filled, some others were doing the same thing. The sergeant shouted to get out of the water and pour out all that we had collected. I quietly slipped my canteen into my canteen holder and marched on. As soon as water was not on the training cadre's mind, I removed my canteen, put a purification pill into it, and took a drink. I passed it around until it was empty.

We marched all night. Upon arrival at the camp, we were advised that the mess hall was serving pork chops, gravy, and eggs. Almost everyone was so tired that they went immediately to bed without eating, but not me! Those were the best pork chops. I think I ate five of them.

Another day we were training to use and qualify on the machine gun. At the end of the day, they decided to leave the gun emplacements set up on the course. There were only about twenty emplacements, and only twenty soldiers could qualify at a time, so not all of our company was able to qualify the first day. We needed the remaining men to qualify the next day. They told me and three other soldiers to stay there to guard the equipment.

The area was home to mountain lions and wild hogs, but I felt comfortable being there with three heavily armed comrades. When the machine guns are loaded, the gunner must operate the bolt until at least one round of ammunition goes through the gun un-fired. This machine gun characteristic left many rounds lying at each station. When the four of us were alone, we went to the firing stations and picked up plenty of rounds to use in our rifles, which used the same kind of ammunition.

At dinnertime, a jeep arrived with our meal. I recognized one of the deliverymen. I addressed him by name, and his response was, "Where do I know you from?" I replied that I knew him from grade school back in Oklahoma, twelve years ago. He could not remember me, but he acknowledged that he had been there back then. He said that he had lived in California for almost twelve years and was surprised that I remembered him or his name.

After a month or so, our training was completed in Hunter Leggett Military Reservation, and it was announced that we would be marching out of the mountains. They said it would be a 56-mile march up and down mountains. They cautioned us about the need to take care of our feet by washing them, powdering them, and changing socks. I listened to the trainers and did just what they said.

I carried a Browning automatic rifle, and they assigned a fellow soldier to carry my ammunition. I had
carried the heavy automatic rifle most of the day when
he said, "You have carried that load all day. Let me carry it awhile." I let him have it for maybe forty-five minutes. When I noticed him limping, I took it back. At
this point we had traveled down a mountain and up
and down the second one. The march up the second
mountain was on a road with accompanying jeeps. The
jeep odometers registered seventeen miles up the final
climb. The former mountain only had had a goat trail,
so we had no way of determining how many miles we
had traveled.

After dark we arrived at the area where we would
be spending the night. This friend who had carried the
weapon for a while suggested that we tent together. I
consented to do that. He was carefully removing his
boots, so I looked at his feet. All the skin had come off
the bottoms. His boots were wet with blood and clear
fluid. I said, "You have to get those feet medicated," but
he refused to do it. The next morning, he delicately put

his shoes on and began the trip down the same mountain we climbed the night before. When walking downhill, your feet slides to the toe of your shoes, making it a lot more painful on sore feet. It hurt me to watch him walk.

The last day of the march, we walked down one mountain. In all, we had walked down one mountain and up and down two more mountains, for a total of fifty-six miles. When we reached our final destination, buses picked us up. We were at the Laguna Seca Race Track. To an Oklahoma young man, the mountains and the snow streams were a memorable experience. I loved being there, even under the military training conditions, but I never could get comfortable bathing in melted snow! Once we were back at the base, each person was processed and sent to their next military assignment. I was only in for six months, so I was discharged back to the National Guard of Oklahoma.

At twenty years old, my life resumed as a civilian, with no college education or qualifications to do any type of skilled labor. Jobs were hard to get if you were not skilled or college educated. I had no money to go to school and no one willing to train me in skilled work. The only opportunity for me was menial labor at a minimum wage. With Dad's help, I got a job where he worked. I did very repetitious steps manufacturing sheet metal parts. This job did not last long, because the work force started organizing a labor union and went on strike. I would not walk the picket line because my dad continued to work. Since he had helped me get hired at this facility and he did not strike, I chose to simply be unemployed again. Another reason I would not cross the picket line was because I felt my coworkers had a valid point in their quest to gain equity in pay scales.

The next thing I tried was building a go-cart track. Again with Dad's help, I was able to borrow enough money to get into this business. It went well for a little while, but the popularity in go-carts was short-lived, and Dad and I lost money. It pained me that I had caused Mom and Dad more grief.

I was disappointed the go-cart business did not pan

out, but I did get an education in the business world. I guess I simply learned how cruel the world could be. No matter how hard you work or how much desire you have to succeed, sometimes you simply cannot. This experience made me realize I needed to be more cautious about any business venture I tried. Most importantly, it made me realize that I had a great desire to succeed financially. I was tired of being economically substandard.

June and I on our wedding day

At this time I was dating a girl named June, who became my lifetime mate. She and I soon married and started something that is a part of God's plan to make our lives meaningful: a family. One of the best things that happened was when we were blessed with a baby boy a little over a year after our marriage. Then, no less enjoyable, two years later a baby girl was born into our family. My wife was in agreement with me on the fact that raising a family was the most important activity in our lives. We had both been working before we had children, but when our son was born, June quit her job.

June's family gave us five acres of land, and we started planning to build a new house on it. My best friend drew up some plans that were laid out like we wanted. He drew a foundation plan, a floor plan, and an elevation view of the planned house. Then we took the plans to suppliers to get quotes for the materials needed. After we knew the cost of building the house, we arranged for a loan and the building began. June's family and I supplied most of the labor, and it took about eight months to build.

When the house was completed, the banker who loaned us the money came out to see it. He was impressed, and he asked me to go into the house-building

business with him. He knew the cost and saw the finished product, but he didn't know about all the free
labor. I was tired of carpentry work and turned him
down.

The first house we built and owned.

We set up our loan to be paid off in five years. The
payment schedule was almost more than we could
handle. It took more than half of my paycheck to
make this payment. Living on less than one-half of my
income, however, was something June and I agreed
upon in order to pay off the loan on our home. Our
only unnecessary spending was to go to a local drive-in
for hamburgers on paydays.

This period of time was satisfying but not easy. Our
frugal habits allowed us to have extra money later to

invest in moneymaking ventures, and the proceeds from our investments are what we are now enjoying. Today I think, *What would have been better: to enjoy small amounts when we were younger or large amounts later in life?* I guess it's up to each individual. The downside of doing it the way we did is that there are people we love who chose to spend all their earnings while they were young. Now, they are struggling to survive in retirement, and it hurts to see some of our friends and family in need. Most of them will not let you help them much. The consequence is that we help strangers more than family or acquaintances.

June and I soon found out that our economic goals were different. They weren't even close to being the same, and her attitude became a difficult obstacle for me to overcome. The underlying difference was that she felt almost the opposite about being ordinary. She was completely happy with my making a modest living and had no expectation of luxury. That would seem like it was beneficial to me, as the provider, but her attitude provided no encouragement for me to excel or work for any extra investment income. It almost left me striving alone to achieve what I considered to be economic success. In a good, sound, love-based marriage, those kinds of differences are something that can be dealt with. We eventually did work it out, but it took some time.

It didn't help that my first business project failed, and June had helped me pay the debt. After we were able to finish paying off our home and had saved a little money, I approached her about investing in a business that would meet the needs of many people. I realized the public needed storage buildings. I did not know what to call them, but I knew the Tulsa people needed more storage facilities. I thought we might be able to satisfy this need with a small investment of time and money. June disagreed. She did not see this opportunity and restrained me. A couple of years later, others saw the same need and built what they called mini-storage facilities. As this idea went nationwide, I pointed out to June that we had missed a blessing by not following through with this idea.

Not easily discouraged, the next idea occurred about ten years later. I suggested that we could make some extra money by capitalizing on the fact that the aircraft industry was in a slump. The workers were being laid off in large numbers. Many of these workers had purchased houses on twenty-year notes. These houses were about half paid off, and they were purchased when the interest rate was very low. I took her to look at some of them and pointed out that we had enough savings to purchase dozens of them with a small down payment and assuming the loans on the houses. The payments were low enough that we could rent them out and make a profit while paying off the loan.

June still did not want more than what we had. Simply put, she was satisfied with the status quo. I felt like it was hard enough to fight in the business world, and doing it alone would be an overload. So I decided not to do it at all. Later these homes increased in value about ten-fold, at which time I told her we missed it again by not investing in the aircraft workers' homes. Now I was batting two out of three!

CHAPTER 5

From Labor to Management

During almost all of the years we were married, I had a good-paying job and my income covered our needs. I worked hard in a cement plant, and my first assignment was to clean up bulk product that had spilled on the floors of the buildings. This plant was massive. In those early years, the company labor force voted to go union, and there were about eighty of us. After I had worked a few years, I held the offices of steward, vice president, and president of the local labor union.

The cement plant where I worked for many years.

I always felt like any employee owed his employer loyalty and the best effort to get the job done. I advocated doing as good a job as possible, earning the company all the profit we possibly could. I knew that if the company earned a dollar, we had a chance of getting a part of that dollar. If the company did not make a profit, then we would suffer economically. With the size of the plant owner's investment, I felt we had a good chance of having a lucrative career if we did our job efficiently. This was a new plant and had the potential of being very profitable.

In today's dollars, the cost of construction of this plant would be in excess of a billion dollars. It had large processing machines that produced the dust called cement. A simple explanation of what we did was to take limestone rock and other components, either out of the ground or purchased and hauled into the plant, then proportionally mix, dry, and grind these materials into powder. Then we put the powdered mixture through a firing process that chemically changed it, so that when water was added, it could be poured and would harden into concrete.

The cement plant people were copycats. They simply manufactured cement the same way it had always been done, and I recognized it to be a crude process. As a sharecropper's son, I had learned to think of better and more efficient ways of getting jobs done. The first plant modification I recommended was very simple. My job was to shovel spills from the conveyor belt off the floor. I did this several days before I got up enough nerve to do something about the needless spills.

I asked the superintendent of production to come over to where I was working. When he arrived, I pointed out that if we built a catch-pan with a chute to a lower belt, which had the same product on it, no more clean up would be needed at that location. He implemented my suggestion, and I enjoyed a little attention for that improvement. I made other suggestions that also helped our process.

When workers labor side-by-side, pulling together for a common goal, you earn respect for each other. You soon realize that each one of you has abilities needed to accomplish the desired result, and you can rely on each other for your special skills. This kind of respect and trust makes for good relationships in the workplace.

Some coworkers possess different kinds of skills, such as welders, riggers, millwrights, mechanics, and repairmen. A lot of these men are very successful. They have applied their skills for many years for a number of employers. If they are paid well, are frugal with their earnings, and have invested wisely, they may accumulate a lot of wealth.

I became friends with a man who exactly fit this description. He had bought stocks in successful companies when they were in their infancy. The value of some of his investments had increased by factors of hundreds. He owned several houses and had three motor homes. I'm sure he had other wealth that I knew nothing about. I worked with him for twenty years and loved him and his wife.

He shared a story about one of his vacations. He went to a horseracing track named Ruidoso Downs. He loved to watch horse races and bet on them. He would take one of his motor homes to a racetrack and stay until the races were completed. One day he was in the lounge, and an old man came in and announced that the drinks were on him because his horse had won the million-dollar race. He said he was from St Louis, where people called him a junk dealer. However, when he wanted to buy something, the seller did not ask him how he earned the money. They simply asked if he had the money, and he said, "I've got it." This impressed my friend.

One morning this friend of mine came to work and told me his arm was hurting. He said he did not know how he hurt it, but he could not use it. He had been talking about retiring and traveling on the horseracing circuit. He was old enough and had plenty of money to do anything he wanted to do. He had worked his whole life with the idea of quitting early enough to enjoy his life following horseracing.

He was a tough man, but the next morning he came in to work still carrying his arm. The third day people tried to get him to go to see a doctor. The fourth day he did not come to work. He had been taken to the hospital, where he died. Just think: A lifetime of saving and planning for the future that was not to be. I lost a very close friend whom I still miss. I don't know if he knew Jesus, but I do know he will meet Him on Judgment Day.

One day the plant manager came by my workstation. I called out to him, and he stopped to talk to me. I said that I had a suggestion. He said, "You have another one, do you?" I replied yes. I suppose I had a reputation of being a little different from most employees. I told him that before I made this suggestion, I wanted him to promise me something. He said, "Oh, you're getting greedy."

I said, "No, I'm not."

Then he said, "Yes, you are, but that's all right. What do you want me to promise you?"

I said, "If you do not use this suggestion, I want you to personally come to me and explain why the suggestion was not used."

He said, "I promise I'll do that. Now what is your

suggestion?"

I said, "We have many electrically driven pieces of machinery, where the drive systems are placed away from the hot areas by using large chains, much like bicycle chains. When our industry first started using this strategy to protect the equipment from the heat, they had no choice. Today we do have a choice, because we now have high temperature lubricants, seals, and couplings. The chain components shut us down frequently, costing us production and added maintenance. I believe we have fifty or more applications needing this change." He told me he understood and would check this out and get back with me.

I didn't hear from him for six months. Then one day he showed up to talk about my suggestion. He told me that he had written it up and sent it to an engineering firm in Chicago. That day, he had received an answer from them. They recommended we start converting these drives to direct drives immediately, eliminating the chains. The engineering company said that the modifications would result in about 5 percent savings in power cost. They went on to say that only the plant personnel could determine how much downtime would be eliminated. They also were sure it would be a significant improvement in uptime.

The manager said, "We are forming a crew to do the conversions, and I want you to be the supervisor over the undertaking."

My reply was, "I'm a husband, I'm a father, I'm an employee, and I'm a student going to night school. I have no more room in my life for additional responsibilities. You have a lot of people in the maintenance department that are very capable and will make you a good leader for the new crew." A short time later the plant picked one of my friends to supervise the construction of the drive relocations.

Later on in our conversations, he asked me what I planned to do with this education when I completed it. My response was, "I would like to become the plant engineer, so that I can do what I love to do all the time, which is improving the plant."

He said, "I understand, and the management determined the changes that emerged from this suggestion will mean millions of dollars in savings and increased production. Management insists you allow them to compensate you some token amount to show their appreciation." He said they could send my wife and me on a cruise, buy my children some savings bonds, or some other compensation I may want. My reply to this offer was that we were private, rural people and were not interested in traveling. I didn't say it, but the truth was, I worked long hours at the plant, then went home to attend to my husband and father duties, as well as studying for my classes.

After listening to my response, he instructed me to think about what I would like the company to do to show their appreciation. I agreed to think about it and discuss this matter further the next day. The determined manager was at my workstation the next day expecting an answer from me. I stated that I had given the subject some thought. I told him I was attending engineering school at the University of Tulsa, and my request was for him to cooperate with me by adjusting my work schedule so I could attend needed classes that were offered infrequently.

He said, "I will cooperate with you on that request, but that will not change my position on compensation."

I said, "The tuition at this private university is very expensive, and so are the required books. Could I possibly get the company to allow me to enroll in the company tuition and book reimbursement program?"

He said, "I should have known you would come up with something like this." The benefit program was for management personnel only, and it was a worldwide program. He didn't think he would be able to get corporate benefit changes adopted for hourly personnel to be included.

I said, "You asked me to think about what would help me, and this expense burden was all I could think of."

He said, "I will try to get the program changed to include you." In about three months the personnel director came to my workstation and informed me that the company had decided to put me on the staff book and tuition reimbursement program. He went on to say that any other hourly employee would also be allowed to get into the program. I'm sure he did not have a clue as to how this came about. I felt like I was instrumental in helping other workers all over the world, who had enough ambition but maybe not enough money to educationally improve themselves.

Not long after he picked a supervisor to be in charge of the project I had suggested, the planning began. When you have major changes in a production line of machinery, they must be carefully coordinated. After the plan was in place, the plant added a drive conversion crew, whose job was to modify the drives. I was able to go into the plant and see the changes in a number of them. It was very rewarding to see how the company was becoming more efficient, and I felt good about saving the natural resources the Lord had provided for us. Most of these resources are exhaustible and should be used wisely.

At the time these changes occurred, my job title was "repair machinist." It was an important job because many of the critical pieces of machinery had no spare parts on the shelf. When we had an outage and had nothing to repair the broken or worn-out machine, I was directed to find a way to get our production back online. For instance, one day the vibrating feeder above the secondary crusher had broken. This crusher was a 600-horsepower impact-type crusher. To optimize the operation, there was a feeder above the crusher to keep the feed rate even and allow maximum production. This feeder had failed and was shutting the whole crusher down, so they called me.

I went down and looked at the feeder. The pulley on this unit had an off-center hub, and it had come loose. It had run for a while with the pulley spinning on a shaft, which wasn't turning like it should. This destroyed the pulley and the shaft. The loaded rotation wore the bore about one-fourth inch larger than the shaft. The shaft was also worn. This repair was difficult because the feeder moved back and forth about two inches while the motor was stationary. The eccentric location of the hub feature had to be timed with precision so the four belts driving it would remain tight throughout each rotation, and it rotated 1,750 cycles per minute. If the timing was wrong, you could not turn it off quickly enough to save the belts. If we had had a shaft and pulley, we would be down a long time just to pull the shaft and pulley and replace it. But we didn't have any parts.

After I looked at it, they asked if I thought there was any way we could fix it. I said, "Yes, maybe we could make it operational until we can get parts in and do the final repair."

Their next question was, "What do you need to get that done?" I asked for the best mechanic on our plant maintenance crew to bring a handful of flat, bastard files of assorted sizes and a ladder. When he arrived, I gave him a pair of calipers already set to the right size. I wanted him to carefully handwork the shaft to the desired size, making it as round as possible. I told him that while he was preparing the shaft, I would be boring the pulley and making a sleeve to insert into the worn area of the pulley.

A couple of hours later, he had completed his part of the work splendidly. We assembled the feeder drive, carefully timed it, and then fired it up. We successfully secured the rebuilt components so that they remained in place and timed it perfectly. It ran for many years; in fact, I never knew if it ever failed. This repair description is vague and a little bit hard to understand, but it illustrates how many blue-collar workers are required to perform their jobs. There isn't always a clear path to their solutions, and they have to be creative.

Inside the building, where I repaired the 42-inch journal bearing and dust collection system.

One time we ground a huge, rough, 42-inch journal bearing, which had galled to the shaft as it failed. This bearing carried several thousand tons of load while rotating. I'm going to use some engineering terms to explain how these systems worked. These heavy loaded bearing systems must be put together carefully, making the surfaces as smooth as possible. They are made out of metals that are not compatible with each other. The rotating body is usually steel, which has a body-centered crystalline structure. The outside or receiver of this bearing is made out of a metal that has a face-centered crystalline structure. These two types of materials are not compatible. The incompatibility allows the surfaces to move molecules around to develop a more perfect fit. The system uses hydrodynamic lubricating to reduce friction while rotating. The more perfect the surfaces are, the thinner the lubricant can be. The thinner the lubricant, the less shear there is, and less energy is required to turn the moving body.

The self-adjusting characteristic I attempted to explain above allowed our mechanics to hand-grind a less than perfect surface by grinding off all the detected high spots. I set and secured a surface grinder on the bearing pedestal. The unit was returned to production status while we were doing this job. The surface grinder was set and operated with the intention of smoothing the rotating component of this bearing. This reduction had to be uniform and known so the outside component could be manufactured to fit this new diameter. We decided to reduce the thickness of the journal bearing 1/32 of an inch. This was accomplished over a period of forty-eight hours.

While the repair was taking place, management special-ordered a bearing replacement with the correct bore size and had it delivered to our plant. A 1,500-horsepower motor powered the unit. The grinding resulted in some cuttings being carried into the load bearing area of this bearing. I did not worry about this because the cuttings only polished the surface to a more perfect condition. I doubt that the 1,500-horsepower motor turning this unit was loaded a detectable amount by this added polishing. This unorthodox repair saved the company a half a million dollars while producing a finished product. This was a very interesting and challenging job.

One day the same manager who had approved the changes on the direct drives came by and told me that he was offering me the plant engineering job. He told me what it would pay and said that this time he wanted me to take the job he was offering. I responded by saying, "I'm not an engineer. I haven't completed my required courses."

He said, "I once had the engineering job I'm offering you, and I will help you." He went on to say that I would be allowed to attend classes during my workday. If I had my work completed for the day, I could go on home, and I had no certain amount of time to be at work. To accept this job, I had to agree to complete my education. I decided to step up and take the job, and I continued to progress on completing my education as I promised.

I was a little bit uneasy about moving into the job prematurely, but I knew I could help the plant operation by correcting some of the shortcomings of the engineering department. The equipment files kept in this office left something to be desired. I was soon communicating with suppliers of our equipment to get manuals, parts lists, and drawings for existing equipment. I compiled a complete motor listing throughout the plant. This list had all information identifying needed frame, voltage, RPM, size of shaft, key sizes, and usually coupling information.

The plant had hundreds of large drawings with numbers assigned to them, so they could be kept in numerical order and could be easily accessed. I discovered that although people were able to locate the needed information easily, they had trouble replacing the files, manuals, or drawings in the right place. I also kept prints on sticks so dirty hands did not degrade the originals.

Unfortunately, I did not anticipate the reaction from my former coworkers. They viewed me as a turncoat because I had gone from labor to management. I did not get cooperation from some of the hardcore union personnel. The union leadership changed into a body that pulled against the company management instead of cooperating with them. I should add that the compensation received by workers declined as the relationship continued to disintegrate.

Betty Cullum, myself, and Bud Cullum

Once I got my feet on the ground, they gave me more responsibility. They hired an outside contractor named Bud Cullum to do small construction jobs, which were directed by me. Bud soon became a person I could trust to get the job done correctly, and I liked him very much. He had more skills than any man I had ever known in this kind of work. The construction crew addition was employed to enable the plant to keep up with our industry as techniques and new process methods were developed. The changes in the way we bought and installed new and better equipment resulted in noticeable improvements. This separate crew was not subject to maintenance pressures.

My early years of being the plant engineer found me focusing on heat recovery as a way of making the plant more efficient. On a large operation, wasted heat occurred in numerous places. We focused on better heat transfer within the heating units. Also, heat recovery after the hot products leave the processing units is a good place to concentrate engineering attention.

One of the places I focused was any place we had a lot of finished product lost due to spills. I had meaningful success in fuel savings in the shipping department. We loaded several rail cars each week with bulk cement. The hopper cars furnished by the railroad leaked at the lower doors. We used a front-end loader and a dump truck to clean up the spilled material and haul it to the spoils pile. All this wasted energy had to be charged to other tons of product. My solution was to simply spray the door edges with a special liquid that caused the first product loaded to stick to the cracks in the sliding doors. For diligently concentrating on optimizing our production process, we had the lowest energy consumption cost per ton than any time before or after this period of time.

Bulk storage and small locomotive engine

There was another problem at the plant that I was able to address during these years. The problem was also associated with shipping our finished product in bulk rail cars. We had a small locomotive engine to move the rail cars about when filling them. The loading stations only had equipment to fill one end of these rail cars while sitting in the original position. The locomotive engine was required to move each car to load the other end. All this moving of rail cars was expensive and time-consuming.

After studying the loading procedure, I designed a loading chute that would enable the bulk rail cars to be loaded while sitting in one location. I called a manufacturer and commissioned them to build a prototype of this shuttle-type loading equipment. It turned out that this was a worldwide problem in rail loading and ship loading of bulk solids. This company worked out all the details to make my loading chute design meet our needs. They sent me a thank-you letter and a case of whiskey, and they started marketing these chutes all over the world for rail and ship loading. It felt good that my design benefited many people across the globe, those who were loading bulk materials. (I do not drink whiskey, by the way, so I traded it for six packs of soft drinks.)

CHAPTER 6

Family and Fun

Our son Mitchell and daughter Lisa
with June and me

June and I were very involved in raising our children, and the times we raised them in were a lot different than when our parents and grandparents were
raised. Now, it is even more different. Families back
then consisted of a father and mother and several children, and parents believed in disciplining their children. This was because America was a Christian nation,
and most people had read the Bible, where it says that
sparing the rod spoils the child. It also says that if you

don't discipline your child, you hate them, because they will never learn to obey people or God. This will cause them trouble throughout their lives.

The Bible tells us how to discipline them: with love. I believe that if you do not teach your child to obey those in authority over them, you shortchange the child. A child reared with no discipline will likely face much heartache and little success. Setting your child up for failure like that is not showing them love.

I think there is a strong possibility that the poor performance of our public education system is a direct result of our straying away from God's teaching about how to raise our children. Our teachers' inability to pass their knowledge on to their students may not be a flaw in their ability to teach but in the student's ability to listen and obey.

I also think we have allowed our public education to become so secular, that no one even thinks about God while they are being educated. Ever since prayer was taken out of the schools in the early 1960s, our youth have become more and more rebellious, lawless, and reckless. This separation from God has resulted in a downward spiral toward chaos in our nation.

To move away from the proven practices of our elders was irresponsible and has only made many lives miserable. Too many children are out of control and cause nothing but heartache. June and I thank God that we raised Mitchell and Lisa to love God, to respect their authorities, and to listen and obey. We are not perfect, but we have been blessed, have good times together, and have enjoyed a lot of success as a family because we followed the Bible instead of the popular, political culture of our time.

June and I (middle), Mitchell and Stacey (left),
Lisa and Andy (right), and grandchildren
Matthew, Marissa, Stephen, and Keeton

We not only disciplined our children, but we took part in their activities. Like many other families, we were busy with Little League, football, basketball, and band. While in high school, our daughter Lisa was a rifle girl in the band, and she also played clarinet. We attended many of these events. When my children were small, we were faithful to church. We took the children to high school sports events also.

Another interest we pursued was round track racing.

Dan Diaz sedan race car, owned by Chief Eaton

Our area had a small track that raced every Saturday night. My family knew a couple of the participants. Other family members also had an interest in these local races. Sometimes the outing was a family event. My wife's younger brother Jim was one of those people, who followed the local racing. While he was serving in the military, we attended most races and mailed the programs to him in Vietnam, so he could keep up on local racing news. This activity engrained into our son the interest of watching racing. He still goes to local racetracks to enjoy it.

Weekends were sometimes spent doing things for entertainment. I had an idea of how to catch some fish. We had a large creek that entered into the larger river not too far from where we lived. I decided to catch some small perch and put them into a barrel to be used as live bait. I borrowed Dad's boat, which I planned to use on an overnight fishing trip. I got all the prep work done and traveled to the river. When I got there, I unloaded the boat and traveled up the river to start my fishing. I put out thirteen limb lines, baited with several sizes of live perch. Next I set the trotline and baited it. By the time I got all this done, it was getting dark and I was tired, so I laid down to take a short nap.

About two hours later, two men woke me up and asked if I had a white boat. I replied that I did, and they informed me it had just gone down the river.

I said, "How could that happen? I took it completely out of the water."

They said the river suddenly rose about four feet and floated my boat off. They further informed me that they saw it hung up on some rocks a few hundred feet downstream. When I looked at the river, I could not believe how swift and turbulent it had become. These very helpful men walked over this hill, about three hundred yards, and showed me where the boat was located. It was way out in the river, bobbing around against a large rock. I decided to go after it. The men tried to talk me out of it, because it was so dangerous.

I walked upstream and waded as far as I could, then I swam to the boat and got a hold of it. It was difficult, but eventually I was successful in getting it on land. Now I had a borrowed boat in an isolated area, where there was no road to bring the trailer to pick it up. We took the motor off the boat and laid it down on the bank. Then the three of us carried it over the hill, back to my camp. We had to rest a few times, but we were able to get it back on the trailer.

After the boat was recovered, I made another difficult trip over the hill to carry the motor back to the boat. I decided not to fish after dark in the wild flowing river. The next day, I dove down and found where I had tied off the trotline. While raising it up to where I could reach it with my head above the water, I could feel fish pulling on the line. I proceeded to take my catch off the trotline and put them in my live box. As soon as I got through with this chore and was enjoying my catch, I noticed some men running my limb lines. I ran to the wide creek and swam it to stop the fish stealing. I managed to run them to their car, and they left — but they had taken all of the fish from my limb lines. I also discovered there were men stealing fish out of my live well. Needless to say, I went home tired and disappointed, with no fish, never to return to this fishing hole. It was not the entertainment I had had in mind.

One day it was snowing lightly, and I was at home

reading the paper. I scanned the classified ads and noticed a farm for sale. I thought, *Dad is almost retirement age. I wonder if he would like to retire on a farm.* I called and asked the realtor if we could come and look at the farm. He agreed to show it to us, and I tried to get Dad to look at it. He said no, that he had already purchased a rural acreage I knew nothing about. I finally persuaded him to just go look.

When we arrived at the property, we saw it had a pretty good house on it and two ponds. One had no visible water running into it and was overflowing continuously. I told Dad that if he wanted the farm, I would pay one-half of the cost. He got excited and went home to tell Mom about it. Later, I got a call from Mom saying she had called my younger sister and told her about our farm-purchasing activities. She said that my sister wanted in on the action. It all came off as if it was meant to be. We each paid a third, and everybody gained. Mom and Dad got their farm, and my sister and I got the privilege of helping them realize their dream.

My sisters: Treva, Verda, Nona, and me
Treva helped in the farm purchase for our parents.

I told Dad, "I think you should remain here in town until you retire." He listened to me, as usual, and then began to move to the farm as soon as it was available. This meant he had to drive about forty miles to work, but they were living their lives the way they wanted to. I was glad to see their enthusiasm, as they fixed it up and enjoyed their farm. They bought cattle, built a barn, and bought a tractor. They planted food crops for the farm animals, and I believe they loved it.

Sometimes things do not go as planned and disappointments unexpectedly occur. A few years later I got a phone call while I was at work. The person said that

Mom and Dad's house had burned, and no one could find them. They were obviously on the road, because their truck was gone. I made some calls and found them. When they heard what had happened, they were devastated. They were desperate again, with no place to live.

Dad's sister moved their motor home up to the farm, and they lived in it while they decided what to do. Only a week had passed when Mom informed me she was getting claustrophobic living in that motor home. I purchased a mobile home and had it moved up to the farm for them to live in until a conventional home could be completed. My other siblings, my wife, and I bought other household furnishings to help make their life more comfortable.

Steve, Treva, our mother Edith, Rudy,
our father Rudolph, Verda, me, and Nona
The family crew that worked to rebuild our parents' house.

The fire department said they had let it burn to the
ground so they could collect the insurance money, but
they had no insurance on the house. I used my vacation time to help them. They found a very good old
house for sale to be moved. We measured all the dimensions of the house so we could pour footings for
it. We had the mover place the house over the footings,
on the steel beams they used to move it. We then laid
concrete blocks in all places except where the beams
were holding up the house. After the mortar between
the blocks dried, the mover set the house down upon

the foundation. Once the beams were out of our way, we filled in the foundation where the beams had been removed. By the time my vacation was over, we had the house properly sitting on the foundation. Then family and friends began reconditioning it.

The house had to be rewired before any other finish work could be done. Dad did a lot of the wiring, while I was working at the plant. Near the end of the wiring job, I went to help on the project. I arrived at a time when Dad was very frustrated, because he was unable to wire a three-way switch he wanted in the living room. He told me he had worked all day, trying to get the correct wiring combination, and would appreciate some help. In only a few minutes, it was wired and working correctly. He was stunned that I finished it so quickly. I think it had whipped him so badly, he needed to simply lay it down and address it later. Sometimes we need to wait until we can clear our minds and take a fresh look at the problem. If he would have done that, he probably could have completed it himself.

My cousin and I built the outside soffit and brick

pocket work on the whole house in one day. He was a very good — and fast — carpenter. My sisters and Dad insulated the house. A friend, Dad, and I roofed it. When the house was finally completed, it looked like a new house, and the tragedy of the fire had made us stronger.

Before the fire, I had purchased two bricks of ammunition and loaned Dad my favorite pistol. I had told him to shoot until his heart was content. I lost my pistol in the fire and have not been able to find one to replace it. Mom and Dad enjoyed the new, old house and their farm until they became so disabled they could not take care of it. I never regretted being involved in their dream-come-true of owning and operating their farm.

As is apparent, in spite of my Dad's violent actions when I was young, I continued to love him throughout my life and never harbored any negative feelings. When Dad's health did not allow them to remain on the farm, they had to get rid of all farm animals and equipment. He offered to sell me his tractor. It was decided I would pay him $1,200 for it. I used it a few years and decided I needed a new one, so I sold it for $1,800. I immediately drove to their house and gave him the $600 profit.

Fortunately, I prospered more and was able to show my love by supplying services and material blessings. They were old and needed my help frequently. They asked me to build them a porch on their home in the town of Broken Arrow, Oklahoma. I did not do this alone, but I saw that it was built just like they wanted it. Dad saw me using my tools in these building projects, and he expressed the fact he liked certain tools, even though he was not able to use them. He was thrilled when I purchased a few tools for him.

Dad wanted me to help him convert a shop into a rental apartment. I was able and willing to do these kinds of tasks for him. These projects required a lot of my time. Why did I do these jobs for them? Because they were my mother and dad, and I loved them very much. I knew the porch would bring them pleasure and the apartment would bring them badly needed income.

I owned a truck, which I used in my business. It was a nice one and I liked it, but I was in a position where I needed to replace it for tax reasons. I drove it over to my parents' home, parked it, and threw Dad the keys. I have more memories of doing other things for them. Some were short and easy; others were long and hard. I wish they were still here so I could continue to do things for them.

Life rolls on. Dad passed away first, leaving Mother to fend for herself. I did not realize how much he did around their place until he was gone. I wish I could hug Mother today, bless her heart! She was so impatient and helpless. One day she asked me to come over and mow her lawn. When she asked me to do anything, she wanted it done that day not tomorrow. I loaded up my large zero-turning radius lawn mower and hauled it to her house to mow her lawn. When I got through, I went inside, and she informed me I had mowed it too fast. I said, "Mom, does it look good?"

She answered, "Yes, but you mowed it too fast."

One fall I was visiting her, and she wanted me to

till her garden so the weed and grass roots would be exposed to the freezing winter weather and die. I said, "Okay, but I'll be leaving on a trip at nine o'clock tomorrow morning with friends, and I will not be able to do it until later in the week."

She then asked, "Why do I always come last on your list?"

I stated, "This time you will not come last on my list." I went home, about ten o'clock that night I hooked up my trailer and loaded my Troy-Built tiller on it, and then I went to bed. A few hours later, I got up way before daylight and headed to her house. When I arrived, it was still pretty dark, but I was able to see well enough to unload the tiller and begin the tilling. I had worked about an hour and a half when Mom walked across the yard with her cane. I saw her mouth moving, so I knew she was talking to me. I turned the tiller off and heard her ask, "What do you think you are doing?"

"Mom, I know what I'm doing. I'm tilling your garden."

"Well, I wanted it tilled but not at night."

One time she called and asked, "Where's my check?"

I told her I did not know where it was, but we would send her another one. It turned out that when she was returning from the mailbox, she dropped it. Later, a neighbor found it and returned it to her. She was appreciative of all that we did for her, including the monthly check. She showed her love with hugs and other gestures. She especially liked preparing good meals for us to eat when we were there. I sure wish she was here today, so I could continue to do things for her.

I regret not going to church with her on special occasions. She was so close to the Lord and was afraid her loved ones would not be spiritually ready to meet Him. She broke my heart when she was near death. She told me she felt like she was a failure in life because she thought some of her children might be unprepared for the Day of Judgment. If I could live a few of those days over, I would be there to meet her expectations.

If one of my siblings were writing on the subject of doing things for our parents, they would have a list of their own. We were all reared in the same environment, leaving us with similar attitudes and desires. They were also involved in similar types of activities related to helping our parents, whom we all loved. Some of them will not have as long a list as others, because they did not live close to Mom and Dad, but we all have a disposition to help others, and particularly our family.

I was the executor of our parents' estate. We had no problems in sharing fairly its contents, and I am so proud of my living brother and three sisters. Our other brother passed away at the age of thirty-nine, so he was not living when they needed our help. If he had been alive during these times, I believe he also would have helped all he could.

One of the most special gifts to my mother came from her daughters, as she was becoming more dependent on others in her final days. My sisters met most of her needs. Early in the decline of her health, one of them was able to live with her and take care of her. During the last six months of her life, more than one person was needed to assist her. My sisters decided to have two of them present at all times, because she was very helpless. Two of them were married and lived near her.

The solution of placing her in a nursing home was totally unacceptable to all of us. We wanted someone who loved her to care for her. One daughter was living there all of the time. The other two alternated on a two-day schedule. This meant they were away from their husbands half of the time. The sacrifice the husbands made was not easy, but since her passing, this special time my sisters spent with Mom is often talked about when we are together. The experiences are enjoyed over and over by all of us. When we were distributing the material goods of their estate, these sacrifices were taken into consideration.

After she died, one of her neighbors shared with us her memories of Mom. She said Mom would sit on her porch, drinking her tea, and rejoicing in the Lord. What a great legacy Mom and Dad left.

CHAPTER 7

Excellence and Loyalty Pay Off

I remained the plant engineer for several years, even though the plant manager I was so close to moved on to another job. While I oversaw the contractor on the small plant assignments, I was very successful at getting things accomplished, thanks to the talent of the gentleman named Bud, who owned the construction company. On occasion, he and his wife would ask my family out for a special dinner, which both families enjoyed. I told him that someday we would return the favor.

As I had expected, the company decided they could no longer afford to keep Bud's construction company on the payroll. Although they discontinued his employment as a contractor, they asked him to do the same job on staff at the plant. He accepted the job and remained under my direction. The only difference was that the person who picked up the check at the special dinners changed from him to me. It's funny how things work out sometimes.

On one of the Christmas dinner outings after this change, we decided to go to a steakhouse nearby. Bud and his wife Betty lived out of town, so we met at my house to ride together to the restaurant. I'm sure Bud gave a lot of thought as to how to best surprise me with his plan. Everyone was dressed up nicely and ready to have some fun. I knew he was mischievous and expected him to pull something. Everything that happened until we ordered our meal was usual. I might add that he loved lobster.

When the waitress arrived, he told his wife to order steak and lobster. Betty replied, "But I don't like lobster."

Bud said, "Order it, and I'll eat your lobster."

She reluctantly said okay, and then my wife ordered steak and lobster. When it was his turn to order, he ordered steak and lobster. So, of course, I ordered steak and lobster too. I thought, *He's going to get two lobsters, and I will only get one.* So I asked the waitress to bring me a second lobster, at which time Bud spoke up and said, "Bring me another one also." Now he's getting three, and I'm only getting two. His mission was to have more than me, since I was paying the bill. He probably would have ordered any quantity it took to outdo me. We have enjoyed reliving this evening many times. It cost me a lot of money, but it generated so many enjoyable moments afterwards. I got my money's worth! He's not here anymore, and I sure do miss him because I loved that man. My wife and I visit his widow frequently.

Graduation from the Univeristy of Tulsa
June 1, 1975

Still working at the same plant, I kept up my end of the agreement to finish getting my degree. Sometimes the burden of continuing this education effort was difficult to do. I owe a debt of gratitude to June, who helped me all she could. There were times when I needed to study and had little time to do so. Because I had a helpmate who wanted to support me, June made these times as easy as possible.

I remember studying very late at night many times, and she would stay up with me. I would study until I got so sleepy, I was not able to absorb the material. Then I would ask June to let me sleep ten minutes and wake me. Sometimes we did this all night long. I would go to work the next day, and later I would go to school to be tested on the material I had studied the night before. Usually this was during special times, like taking finals.

When I first began attending a junior college, I had been out of high school ten years. I did not make very good grades on some courses. Later, when I was in my last two years of study, I made mostly A's in the courses related to my field. My sister-in-law, Evelyn, was a math major. She was attending the same school and made A's in all of her classes. At the graduation ceremonies, she was recognized as being the top student.

My wife was also attending classes in these same years. Her grade point earned her recognition as being the number two student the same year that Evelyn was number one. Needless to say, I was very proud of these two women, who were onstage at the same time for outstanding performances. I was closer to the *other* end of this grade point scale! These years were a little earlier than my all night studies. I did better when I got into the applied as opposed to the theoretical part of mathematics. Then I rose to the top of the class. I had great enthusiasm and determination to complete my course of study, which would allow me to apply my knowledge in a way that would improve the world I lived in.

One of these applications was a cooling tower installation. I explained to the men I was working with that I was going to use a twelve-inch sewer main to get water back to the cooling tower. They thought I would be unable to do that. The reason they had these thoughts was that all they had ever seen was water flowing in the opposite direction in that line. Since the main pipe was on an incline in the wrong direction, they concluded the water would be unable to flow uphill to the cooling tower.

Another way to explain what I was going to do was to drain the water uphill by building a water column higher than the discharge point. I had done the calculations and determined that the water had to rise to a certain point in the lower manhole before a sufficient quantity of flow would be forced up to the tower. The men were amazed when the water level rose to the point where I had told them it would rise, then flowed back to the tower. This one project made some of my co-workers believe I knew what I was doing when designing systems.

While I was in charge of directing projects of the construction crew, I decided to clean up all airborne dust inside a process building. This included installation of several belt conveyor cleaners, and all of the dust collector systems had to be completely rebuilt. When the work was completed, I stood on a stair landing, where Bud had a good view of most of the building. I said, "Just stand here and look out over the building."

He replied, "What am I supposed to be looking at?"

I simply said, "You could eat your lunch here comfortably. Have you ever seen this building this clean?"

"No I haven't." Mission accomplished and a job well done. The end results made me feel good, and he felt good about his contribution to the project. This kind of success was common with our crew on many projects throughout our facility. These efforts and expenses were justified by not losing the product involved, and the process equipment no longer was exposed to a dirty environment. Another benefit was that the employees had a nice, clean place to do their jobs.

Management often expressed how pleased they were with our performance. One year they told me that they had already given me a pay raise, but they had more money for raises. They said they thought I was the most deserving, and I would be getting an additional raise. Some time passed, and management personnel changed. I got a new boss, and we got a new plant manager. This new plant manager called me into his office and gave me a cell phone. He stated that he had a lot of confidence in my ability to make good decisions, and every fourth weekend I would be required to carry the phone in case on-duty supervisors needed to consult me on critical decisions.

Soon after this occurred, the plant was scheduled to be shut down for a total winter rebuild. Management assigned me to go on a schedule of twelve hours a day and seven days a week for about three months. My responsibility was to assist in the supervision of the maintenance department. I worked all winter on this brutal schedule. A couple of weeks after the winter rebuild was completed, I was back on my regular job and schedule.

After all this sacrifice, my boss told me that if I didn't start working on Saturdays, the new plant manager was going to let me go. I said, "I have been doing my job for many years, and the workload doesn't require that much of my time." I was not going to come to work just to sit and appease him.

My boss said again, "If you don't, he will let you

go." He went to England to corporate headquarters, and while he was gone, the plant manager told me he wanted to see me in his office at four o'clock that Friday. I went to his office at the appointed time, and he terminated me. I was not worried, because years earlier I had started a successful business that would support us well. However, I was puzzled as to why he let me go. I sat at home for about four weeks before I figured out that he was on the take. When I was convinced I was right, I proceeded to get invoices showing just what he was doing. I believe that the reason he wanted to get rid of me was that I was in control of jobs that the company had no idea what the cost should be. On all production jobs that repeated frequently, they knew about what the cost should be.

This man was stealing from them, but I decided I would not say anything to anyone in the company. I probably had a valid legal complaint about losing my long-time job, but also I was thinking about the possibilities of a countersuit. By this time, I had accumulated material wealth that I didn't want to put at risk.

After my boss retuned from England and found out
that the plant manager had terminated me, he was up-
set. He came to my house and promised me that if I
would file a lawsuit, he would testify in my behalf. He
brought paperwork that proved my termination was
unjustified. Furthermore, he was willing to sacrifice his
own job to do this, as he would surely be fired. I decided not to sue a corporation that had unlimited resources. And, being let go freed me from a very stressful
job. I had been eating a roll of antacids about every two
days. I carried them with me for a few weeks after I lost
my job, until I realized I no longer needed them.

After I was unemployed a year or two, I got a phone
call asking for information about the plant facility that
no one knew but me. I told the maintenance superintendent I would be right out and help them solve
their problem. I drove out to the plant and told and
showed them what they needed to know. They tried to
pay me for the services but I refused to take any money. Not long after this first phone call for help, another
situation developed where my help was needed and I

helped them once more. The two instances happened while the plant manager who terminated me was still there.

Four years after my termination, I got a phone call from a man who said he was a private investigator. He said that he had heard I had written evidence that the plant manager was stealing from the company. To this statement my reply was, "Who are you?" The phone got very quiet.

He continued, "You do need to know, don't you?"

I said, "Yes. Who are you working for?"

He said, "Call the corporate office to verify that I'm who I say I am. I'll call you tomorrow."

I wondered if I was being set up for a lawsuit. I called corporate headquarters and found out he was legitimate. He called me the next day, and I shared what I knew about the topic he asked about. He asked me why I had not reported the situation to the corporate office. I replied that I thought I would be viewed as a disgruntled ex-employee. He then said that so much time had passed, he could do nothing for me.

I said, "You called me. I didn't ask you for anything. Don't worry about me. I'm doing okay. But I want you to promise me that the manager will be terminated. I have friends that he has terminated and some of these friends needed their jobs. I had other friends who remained at the plant who may need to keep their jobs. If he remains in control of the plant, he will unjustly discharge others."

He replied, "I promise he will be gone in three months." He kept his promise to me.

About a year after the private investigator contacted me, I got another phone call from plant personnel. They approached me about coming to work as a consultant. This was not offered as a permanent job. I would be a private contractor. I thought about it and agreed to come back for a while if I could earn big bucks. I believed my return would help me feel better about my long-term employment ending abruptly with very few people knowing why. It might even help my image in the eyes of my former coworkers.

The consulting job lasted two years and lined my

pockets quite well. I felt the company knew that I didn't deserve to be terminated. They showed their true character by being a good and fair bunch of people. They offered me my former job back at twice what I was making when I was discharged, but I refused the offer. They simply had waited too long. I loved the freedom of not being obligated to anyone.

Not working for someone else allowed me to focus on what I had been doing independently for about seven years. I didn't make much money until I had enough time to expose myself to business opportunities. Prosperity ensued as I followed the Lord's leading and He blessed me. Another thing that entered into the decision not to sue the company was how good they had been to me over many years. I wanted to show my appreciation for all the good times. I didn't want it to end on a sour note.

My former boss was a good man. I knew I could trust him, and he and I spent a lot of time together. We talked about more than work-related subjects, and he found out that, if you were around me much, sooner or later I would be telling you about the love of Jesus. He said he was agnostic and had no interest in discussing the topic of religion. A few years later, he and his wife got a divorce. He had two sons who suffered much in the following years. Then one of the heartbroken sons shot and killed him.

I often think of how good this man appeared to be. What a shame if he found out too late that there really is an Almighty God, who loved him so much that He sent Jesus His Son to die for his sins. After death, all opportunities for redemption cease, and I can only hope that, in his last moments, he received Jesus as his Lord and Savior. It pains me to think he might be spending his eternity in agony, away from God's goodness and love.

Along these lines, I believe God knows what motivates us. He knew I struggled with poverty and all the heavy burdens I had to bear while growing up. He also knew about my desire to rise financially through business opportunities, so that my family would be comfortable and carefree. Being in the upper income group is a much better place to be, but it requires work and perseverance. God must have put this desire in me, because He has blessed me all along the way.

CHAPTER 8

The Challenges of Doing Business

In 1979, I was still working at the plant and desired to rise above the norm economically. To achieve this, a person must be willing to do what it takes to make this happen. I told June that I wanted us to start our own business and that if she wasn't willing to go along with this idea, I would never bring it up again. This time, she said she would help me. She said she knew I would never be happy unless I tried to get into a business of our own. This was great news, because I knew we could be a success if she and I pulled together.

The business we got into was mobile home parks, which required a lot of capital, so we started small. We bought and rented one mobile home. In about two months we purchased another one, and then later we bought a third. We saved a lot of money because I moved them and set them up myself. Soon we were able to purchase five lots in a mobile home addition, which we filled with rentals. At that point, we had eight rentals. We realized that the workload to manage and maintain all these rentals would soon get to be too much for me to do while working full time at the plant — another good problem to have.

The next step was to purchase a mobile home park of forty-eight spaces. The lots were all full except two. Twenty-four lots included mobile homes on them, which were part of the purchase. Six of these were empty and in bad need of repair. In the beginning, my other rental income was equal to what we were losing on the park. I went to work on the empty houses and rented them. I also announced an increase in the lot rental rate. This stopped the negative cash flow, and this venture paid off better than expected. We had financed it for ten years and were able to pay off the note in only five years. By then, our net worth increased by a factor of ten.

We were soon looking for more property. Our profits from the first park gave us the resources to grow. This venture was educational to me. I learned that some of the occupants of mobile homes live there by choice and have large net worth. Others are not qualified to do skilled jobs and cannot afford large, expensive homes. And there were those who were disabled physically or mentally. I also learned most are humble, kind, likable people. I don't live in a mobile home, but these people are my kind of people.

At that time, other businesses were trying to do the same thing we were doing, and parks sold so quickly, we missed many opportunities. We finally found one forty miles away from where we lived. The long driving distance from our home made this venture less attractive, and it was an old park, but we bought it and were able to make it into a good investment by upgrading it. The lots were sized for smaller mobile homes that were sold at the time it was constructed. This fact alone made the lots more difficult to rent, because homes now were much bigger. The new homes were difficult to place on the small lots.

When you are a businessman, you deal with things as best you can to enable you to reap the most out of your investment. One of the difficulties in making the new park function as it should was that the sewer main's pipes were too small and needed replacement. I got busy upgrading these lines, which were under the existing homes. To do the job, I removed the skirting and crawled under the house to dig by hand the ditches for the new system. It was a hard and dirty task, but a successful businessman must be willing to do whatever it takes to accomplish the desired goal.

One day one of my aunts came by and saw me. She stopped her car and tried to help, but I told her this appeared much worse than it really was, because under a house it was cool, out of the Oklahoma heat. Also, I was conditioned by the tough farm labor of my youth. My aunt still was very concerned and wanted to help me. She had some money and always helped anyone she thought needed it. I thanked her for her offer but refused. By doing this myself, I also made sure it was done right.

This property required many other difficult projects like the one I just described. Most of the gain I enjoyed in life came about because of my willingness to do all that it took to make things work as they should. As a mechanical engineer, I understand what needs to be done to make systems work properly. In fact, all of the properties I have purchased have had deficiencies that the seller was not willing or qualified to correct. Most of the previous owners were not onsite or willing to get their hands dirty to solve their costly problems.

One park I purchased had a water bill almost equal to the total monthly receipts. I walked down the sewer lines, looking into the open drops, until I discovered clean water running down one of the sewer mains. After checking it all hours of the night and day, I was positive this was the problem and started to dig it out. Uncovering the lines revealed a supply line leak, and the lost water was running directly into the main sewer line. It was down so deep that the surface was not damp. I wonder how many thousands of dollars the previous owner had lost because of this.

With all my work and attention to doing things right, however, I still had some losses. One of them was unjust, but I learned how the government can take advantage of you. All it takes is a few government employees who are more interested in getting more money for the government than they are in serving the people who pay their salary. The Internal Revenue Service (IRS) notified me that they were going to audit me. The tax laws allow a deduction for money spent on depreciable rental property, which is depreciated over a defined period. When I began purchasing rental property, the IRS had the added enticement of credits on new purchases of business properties. After the purchase of this mobile home park, I had filed for an investment credit on the lift station serving the park.

When I met with the auditor, she scrutinized all the depreciable property I claimed. Not many changes were required to satisfy her on the depreciation amounts, but she disallowed the entire investment credit I claimed. I simply could not believe what I heard because I knew the law. I said, "Ma'am, lift stations do qualify for these credits. The small business tax guide used lift stations as the example for qualifying investment credits."

She said she didn't care and was disallowing my claim for these credits. When I talked to a tax lawyer about my problem, he said I was absolutely correct. He could assure me of a favorable court victory, but it would take about twice as much money to go to court than I would recover from the IRS, because the tax laws did not order them to pay legal fees if they lost. He also stated that if I sued the IRS, they would probably audit me every year. At this time I was a fledging business-man struggling to meet my financial obligations on financed business properties. I couldn't spend a large sum of money to make the government do what was right, so I took the loss of the investment credits.

When I purchased another mobile home park, I found that the electric power was supplied by a coop-erative requiring membership. This organization was charging so much money for deposits and member-ships, it was causing me to lose many applicants as cus-tomers. They would pick out a lot, pay the first month's rent, contact the electric company, and find out how expensive it was to turn on the power. We would refund their money, and they went to a location that was served by another electric company.

I did a study and found there were ninety-four electric cooperatives in the state of Oklahoma, and this group was the third most expensive. Most of the people in my mobile home park could not afford expensive fees. They were first-time homeowners, usually recently married and starting a family. When I appealed to the good-hearted nature of the electric cooperative, I found out they didn't have a heart. They turned a deaf ear to my plea for relief for these people.

After I asked for relief from both individual board members and the entire board, my attitude changed. Instead of pleading, I demanded they lower their fees and deposits. I told them, "You are hurting the young families, and I am going to stand up for them as well as myself. I know all the areas you serve, and I know you are oppressive in the way you do business. If you don't change to more acceptable practices, I'm going to start running advertisements in all the newspapers in your service areas, telling the public about the unfair economic requirements you impose on the public." In only a few days, they decided to lower their membership fees and deposits.

This same cooperative has above ground secondary service lines all over our park. One day we had a storm and suffered some tree damage in one location. A tree was pressing the electric line down, and it was touching a mobile home. The electric company had suffered damage all over their service area. When I went out there to assess my damage, I saw the children of the park climbing into the tree that was leaning on the power line. Immediately I got my saw and cut it down. I tried not to damage the service line, but the tree rolled and did additional damage to the line. Now I had a hot wire on the ground. I called the power company and told them about the dangerous situation, and they soon arrived. In about four hours they were able to mend and restore the broken line.

In a month I received a bill for $1,520. I called and asked why I had been billed. They informed me it was for the damage I caused on their power line. I asked,

"Am I responsible for acts of God? A storm caused most of the damage." They said I would have to pay the bill, so I requested a list of everything they did and how much they charged. A large percentage was to replace damaged breaker boxes on lots adjacent to the tree. I said that if I was required to pay for all of these broken boxes, I wanted them. They said they had thrown them away.

They didn't know it, but I had examined these three boxes and found they had no damage and were still on the poles. I told them this and said I was not going to pay for their replacement. The next month I received another bill that was one-tenth of the original bill. I let them know I owed them nothing and told them not to send me any more bills. They issued notices threatening to turn off my power.

The Corporation Commission regulates our utilities, so I called them and asked about charges for damages. I learned what a utility company could and could not do. I found out they could only sue me for the money for the alleged damages. They were not allowed to turn off my power for anything except not paying my electric bill.

I called the electric cooperative and asked them to sue me. "I would love to get you in court, so I can tell the court and the public how you treat your customers." For eleven months each electric bill was accompanied with a notice that they were going to cut off my power. When I received the eleventh one, I again called the Corporation Commission and informed them I was still getting cut-off notices. I said, "If it is illegal to turn off the user's power, then it should be illegal for them to threaten to do so."

After this phone call, the president of the electric supplier invited me to his office, where he apologized for their actions. He requested that in the future I call them when a tree caused problems. About six months later, a large tree split and hung over their power line. I immediately called them, and the field supervisor came out and asked where the problem was. I told him, and a few minutes later he came back to tell me they would let the tree fall on its own. It would be my responsibility to clean up afterward. However, they would repair the power line.

I told the supervisor that management had promised they would take care of these kinds of situations. He said, "We will do as we say," and he left. I went to the phone and called the president of the power company and explained what had just happened. He said, "Okay, I'll take care of it." Shortly afterward, the field supervisor knocked on my door again. He wanted to know where I wanted them to stack the wood and put the wood chips!

Sometimes I feel like I must fix some of our flawed systems in business and government. I believe it's hardest to get a fair shake from our government agencies, primarily because our laws protect government employees when they do wrong. They are not held accountable for their actions. For example, every month I was required by regulations to collect water samples and have them tested to insure the safety of my park occupants. The Oklahoma State Health Department laboratory tested my samples and they passed every month. I was charged for their services.

In June the government sent me a notice that I had missed the March test, that I must collect samples and have them tested or I would be subject to a $10,000-a-day fine. I informed them, "I have already done the samples each month, and you tested them and they passed. You need to get your act together." I couldn't believe it when they did the same thing in April. Again, I set them straight. Sometimes our government can be so disorganized and unprofessional. I will point out that every time they run a small rental business out of business, it simply moves more people into the government projects.

One night on television I watched an auction of properties offered by liquidators of a failed savings and loan business. To my surprise, they offered four lots in a mobile home addition. I didn't have a bid number and couldn't bid on them, but the next day I contacted the law firm that was liquidating the assets. I asked what the four mobile home lots brought. They replied that they didn't sell them and that there were forty-three of them. I asked what they wanted for them. They said they wanted $3,200 per lot. My next question was how much earnest money was required. They informed me they needed $25,500. I told them to write up the contract and do the title work. I was bringing them the earnest money for the purchase of all the lots.

When I arrived at the law office, they took my money and gave me a contract defining the terms of the sale. I signed the contract for the purchase of the lots at their price. I informed them I was going to be out of town for a few days and would get back with them the following week. When I returned home, my phone recorder had a message on it saying they were going to auction off the lots I had purchased. I called to remind them that we already had an agreement. They said they were going to auction them off at two o'clock Thursday.

I said, "If you are that unethical in doing business, I will not be there."

Their response was, "You will be there."

After I hung up the phone, I got another phone call from a man, who said, "I hear we will be bidding against each other tomorrow on some lots."

I said, "I don't think so. I've already bought those lots." I explained what had occurred.

He said, "I did the same thing two days after you did! So what would you charge me for you to stay home?"

"For ten thousand dollars I will not be there."

He said, "I'll give you $7,500."

I said, "You got a deal." I wasn't going anyway. Why not earn a good payment doing what I was going to do for free? Not long after the auction on Thursday, he asked me to come to his office, where he paid me.

About two years after the lots were sold to the other gentleman, I received a call from him stating that he would like to sell his remaining lots to me. He had sold some of them but still owned thirty. He stated that he did not need to make very much money on the lots. I told him I had purchased another mobile home park since we last talked. I went on to say that my wife and I were mowing about as many empty lots as we wanted to at this time. About a year later, I received another call from him asking if I would buy the lots at the price he paid for them. My response was, "Thanks, but no thanks."

After another six months he called me once more. This time he was different. He asked me if I could come down to his home and talk to him. I told him I could do that, but I didn't want to buy those lots. He said, "Please come on down and talk to me about buying the lots. I've got cancer, and I'm only expected to live thirty days. If you would buy the lots I can die in peace. You will do good with them. My wife does not have a clue as to what should be done with them."

My response was, "I'll be right down." I decided I should step up and help him out. He was in such a bad spot and really needed my help. I wrote up a simple contract for us to sign. I traveled to his home and visited with him for a little while. I shared with him the fact that I had written a contract defining the terms of the purchase. This instrument stated that I would purchase the lots at the price he paid for them. It stated he would furnish marketable title and abstracts at closing. I was to pay one half of the agreed price at closing. I explained to him that I did not have enough ready cash to pay the full amount immediately. We agreed I would pay half at closing and the remainder in six months. I then witnessed to him about God's love for him and His willingness to redeem him, and we prayed together. I believe God saved his soul!

Before the titles were prepared, I received a phone call from his son telling me he had passed away. A few days after he was buried, I received another phone call from the son asking me if there was any way I could pay the whole amount at closing. He said if I could, they were willing to discount the amount about seven thousand dollars. I agreed to do that. A couple of days later, he called to say that the abstract company wanted almost $6,000 to prepare the necessary title records. I said, "Well, when I sell them, I will have to spend that same amount. But I'm willing to do the deal if I could keep $4,500 to cover my costs when the lots are sold. This will save you $1,500. Under the new contract conditions, I will pay the full amount of the purchase price, and I will drop the abstract requirement." We agreed, and it was a done deal.

When I took possession of these properties, I dropped the rental rate down very low. The rate I decided on was about half the market price. Word soon got around, and they began to fill up. The renters knew what a good deal that was. They also knew I would not keep the rental rate low for a long period of time. The low rates were low enough to cut the renters some slack when they really needed it. I was compassionate and purchased property that I really did not want, and God saw this. I believe He rewards us for doing unselfish deeds such as this one.

Before I left my job at the plant, I had bought a piece of property that had been zoned to be developed as a mobile home park. I looked into the legal aspects and the availability of utilities. The location of the utilities greatly impacts the cost of acquiring and constructing a development. The developer looks at the cost of bringing utilities to the property and must be able to get approvals from the providers. The approvals are more a function of politics than anything else. Sometimes individuals and corporations have unlimited monetary resources, and they will use them to oppose you. That was what I encountered after I purchased this development property.

I took the preliminary steps to build the new mobile home park, and a local man sued me. He owned a large oil company and was seeking an injunction to stop me. As wealthy as he was, the court ruled in my favor. My next move was to ask the local sewer utility if I could use their service, but they denied me, and you cannot force a utility to allow you to use their services. However, I was not without legal options.

I got approval on a water supply from a rural water district, which was assigned by the federal government to serve this area. I had a right to build my own sewer system if I built it by state standards. I was required by law to hire a qualified company to design the system. During this period of time an opposition group was having planning meetings, strategizing on how to stop my project.

I went ahead and hired a company to design a sewer

system that met state standards. The plan had to be approved by county and state officials before the system could be built. After I submitted the plan, I received a call from the engineering company stating that we had been turned down. They said I had a legal problem not an engineering problem.

I conferred with my lawyer to see what I should do next. He asked me if there were any other designs we could use to take care of the waste disposal. We went through these steps two more times, seeking approval from the county, but all our efforts were unsuccessful. Even though all three of the designed systems met the requirements, they were turned down.

The only thing left for me to do was to seek a legal solution to my problem. The legal steps on alleged denial of one's rights involve discovery sessions with all parties involved. I was in a position where I had to continue to try to find an equitable solution to my venture. I was still doing well financially, but this legal process had been going on for a few years. Finally, I could see it winding down.

We were scheduled to appear in court when the new plant manager at my job decided that he no longer needed my services. This mobile home venture was another reason my leaving was perfect timing. It enabled me to dedicate a lot of time to prepare for the upcoming court date. I ordered a book from the U.S. Geological Survey, because the discovery sessions revealed they were claiming our project would adversely impact the environment. The underlying stone would dissolve and let the sewer water enter the water table if my sewer system was built.

I studied the makeup of the earth in our area. My purpose was to assess the impact of my development on our environment. However, by digging into the topic of environmental impact, I discovered that the county was doing the same thing they did not want me to do — within three miles of my proposed project. What they were doing involved treating the same kind of waste with the same type of process. The only difference was that the concentrations in their facility were *hundreds of times more* than mine would be! And, their system was built over the same rock formation. I also determined they had approved four thousand septic systems in the same area. These systems were using a much more undesirable way to get rid of human waste.

The county was treating thousands of times more waste, both residential and industrial. Their facility was the same type I was planning to build. Their legal position was based on the alleged concern that my system would contaminate the water table. The obvious question was: Why were they concerned about my *small* facility contaminating the underground water and not concerned about their *huge* facility doing the same thing, since it was located over the same geological formation?

They had *seven large* treatment cells. I applied for *one small* treatment cell. We now had proof that my plans were illegally denied. I worked many hours uncovering their true character, and I informed my attorney of the facts. He took this information and other previously known facts and masterfully defeated a much larger group of county defense lawyers. In fact, he intimidated the county defense team at the very beginning, when they were picking the jury.

Eighteen potential jurors were directed to stand up and tell the court their name, home address, and vocation. When this was completed, my attorney was allowed to question them. He had committed all their information to memory and knew everyone's name, where they lived, and what they did for a living. He took no notes and made no mistakes. It amazed everyone in the courtroom. When the defense attorney took the floor, she simply told the court she did not know anyone's name or where they lived or their vocation.

The case lasted five days, and my attorney never relinquished control. He was so entertaining, the jury would scoot out to the edge of their seats, their eyes fastened on him. When the county lawyer was speaking, it was obvious that they were not captivated with his presentation. It seemed to me, there was no doubt about who was going to win the lawsuit.

Early on, when the case was being developed, there were times I was discouraged. It seemed like everything that happened cost me money. But I felt that I must continue because of what was at stake. If for no other reason, to throw in the towel would have encouraged these ruthless people to run roughshod over other business people. I also had a portion of my life's gain at risk. At one point it was so frustrating that June wanted me to quit fighting them, but I felt I had to get justice.

In the end, the county paid for all proven damages plus interest and legal fees. When the jury foreman passed by my attorney, he shook his hand and said, "If I ever need the services of an attorney, I hope you will work for me."

Was it worth it? Probably not. But it was the right thing to do. I believe we should serve the Lord in this way, with as much determination as we can possibly muster. We serve Him by doing what's right, and I hope my perseverance in this civil case will encourage others not to give up when they face overwhelming odds.

CHAPTER 9

Land and a Beautiful Home

When I began to run my own businesses, I started
to think more about the Lord. I felt as though I needed
a deeper walk with Him. Thinking like this makes you
less selfish and self-centered, and it also motivates you
to read and study the Bible, which is the Word of God.

I asked the Lord to give me a desire to read His
Word and help me grow as a Christian, and soon I was
reading daily and enjoying it. God knows exactly what
each individual can handle in this life. I believe that
He allowed material wealth to begin to flow into our
possession because He knew what we would do with it.
June and I had three parents who were living on small
income streams. We found that nothing was more rewarding than sending monthly checks to our parents
for about twenty years. We have also been blessed to
help others, and we noticed that the more we helped
others, the more God gave us.

One day I called a man who had some property he wanted to sell. The property was contiguous with property we already owned. I asked him how much he wanted for his twenty-five acres. He told me he wanted $185,000 for it. This property was very well located and beautiful, virgin land. I said, "I'm interested in it but not at that price."

He asked, "What would you give for it?"

I said, "Let me think about it and find out how much I have available to spend. I'll call you back tomorrow."

The next day I called and told him I would give him $125,000 for it. His reply was, "Thanks for the offer, but no thanks."

A year later he called to say he wanted to take me up on my offer to buy his land. I replied, "You can't turn down an offer then wait this long and expect me to still have the offer on the table. My economic position and interest changes too much in a short period of time."

He asked, "How much will you pay for the property

at this time?"

My reply was, "Let me think about it and check on how much money I have available."

The next day I called him and told him I would give him $100,000 for it. He said he was refusing the offer and hung up the phone. About a year later he called me and said he was going to take me up on my last offer! I said, "When are you going to understand that offers expire when you turn them down?"

He asked, "Are you saying you will not pay $100,000 for my property?"

I said, "Yes, exactly. My interest and ability to pay changes."

Next question he asked was, "What will you pay for my property today?"

Once again, I said I would call him the next day with my answer. This time I told him I would pay $70,000 for it. His reply was, "I will call you back in a few minutes." Shortly he called me back and asked if I could raise my offer to $75,000.

I said, "Yes, if you can wait three months for the last $5,000."

He replied, "I'll take it."

What makes this sad for him is the interest rates on savings paid by the banks were fairly high at that time. If he had accepted my original offer and put the money into savings, the interest and principal would have accumulated to a figure close to his initial asking price. I purchased the property and took legal steps to have it placed into the city limits of a growing town adjacent to it. I have it listed today with a realtor for more than a million dollars. I haven't sold it at this writing, but I've had an offer of ten times what I paid for it, which I rejected. Although my dealings with the man were a little frustrating a times, in the end I saw how God gave me a great financial gain.

Another similar transaction occurred during the same period of time. June's cousin married a young man named Tom, who was to become a lawyer after his education was finished. I got to know this young man, saw that he was a person who had values and principles I liked, and I wanted to be his friend. At the time I did not realize what a positive impact he would have on my life. In a very short period of time, he developed a thriving real estate law practice. He did an excellent job of handling other legal matters for his customers, but over time he had a reputation of being the best lawyer a person could hire when doing land transactions, because he consistently got everything right on land title opinions. I also observed that that was what he liked to do. Usually, if you like doing something, you're good at it.

His chosen area of law exposed him to many attractive business opportunities. One day we were talking, and he invited me to buy a portion of lake property. It worked out well for me. We only owned it for a short time, and when we sold it we made a good return on the investment. This was just one of many investment opportunities he was involved in all over this area of the country.

I do not know all the details driving him to offer me this next deal, but Tom called me and asked if I would be interested in acquiring an eighty-acre tract of land near my home. He said if I would pay him $25,000 and take over his loan, he would sell it to me. I told him I wanted to do it and followed his instructions. I contacted the bank and told them I wanted to take over Tom's loan, which the bank representative confirmed I could do. He added that I would have to have other property mortgaged along with the mortgage on the property I was attempting to buy. I informed him I was willing to do that if they would allow me to take over Tom's loan and get the same interest rate. He said that to do that, I must get an appraisal on the added property to be mortgaged. The appraisal cost me $800.

A few days later Tom called because I had not assumed his loan. I told him what had happened, and he said, "They are not cooperating with you."

Then I said, "They promised they would let me do that."

Tom said, "I wish I had the money to pay it off."

I said, "If you can still do that, come to my home and get a check and go pay it off."

He was astonished and said, "Thank you! I will take a great deal of pleasure in taking these unethical people completely out of the picture."

When he was at the bank, paying off his loan, the bank called me and said they had money set aside for the loan. I replied, "You lied to me. You told me I would be allowed to take over Tom's loan." The representative of the bank said he was overruled and could not keep his promise. I said, "Tell your bank that I said I do not need to use their money today and furthermore I will never need any of their money."

About a year after I purchased the eighty acres from Tom, he called and asked if I would be interested in trading that land for an eighty-acre track next to the ten acres where I lived. My answer was yes! He proceeded to tell me he thought I could trade if I was willing to pay the $32,000 difference. I told him to go ahead and do the deal, but I wanted a road easement to a farm-to-market road north of the property. He called me back and said the easement requirement was preventing the trade, so I dropped the easement requirement. Tom's next call was for me to bring him the check.

I had purchased other properties, but none were

close to where I lived, and so this purchase was special. It is wonderful to go out on the land and enjoy it. In a few months Tom called me and asked if I would like to buy the land lying between my eighty acres and the farm-to-market road north to my property. I did because that was the piece of land where I wanted a road easement. I would have access for more than a quarter of a mile all along this road. I asked, "How much will it cost me?"

Tom replied, "It will cost you $75,000."

"Buy it for me. I'll have the check ready when you need it."

I greatly appreciated Tom's help in investing in real estate. He was instrumental in helping me grow economically. Tom also has a son-in-law who is an attorney, and I would like to commend him for one unselfish act. John is a civil lawyer in Houston, Texas. He answered a call from the Innocence Project in New York City about a man wrongfully convicted by the State of Texas for the murder of his wife. The man's defense lawyers believed prosecutors had withheld evidence that would have proved his innocence. This man had already served eighteen years in prison, and John labored pro bono for seven years before he was able to force the prosecutors to turn over the evidence and set this man free. Also, because of the evidence John got released, the real killer is now serving time for this crime.

I wonder what will happen to those who did wrong and cost this innocent man twenty-five years of his life. The Bible says that we reap what we sow. Most likely, if they don't repent and give their lives to God, they will have a hard time of it, now and for eternity. But I have no doubt that John and his family will gain great rewards, because the Bible says that we will reap what we sow. These are God's promises. You can count on them.

By the time we were in our fifties, June and I had acquired enough land to make a four wheeler useful as rough terrain transportation. We decided to purchase a farm-style four wheeler. She and I rode it together, and when our grandchildren visited us, it was especially enjoyed. After a few months we decided that a

Land owner, but country boy through and through

purchase of a second four wheeler might be a good move. I told June, "If we buy it, you will have to learn to drive it," so at the age of fifty-seven she learned and soon was comfortable riding it anywhere on the farm. I was proud of her performance as an off-road rider. Sometimes she made me hurry to keep up with her! She's a careful rider but not timid while maneuvering through the forest. Hers was smaller than mine, and she could pass through narrower openings. This was a wonderful way of enjoying God's beautiful creation.

Before I began to study the Bible, I believed that He

was not involved in the daily activities of our lives, but I soon saw that God is sculpturing our lives mostly in subtle ways. I became convinced that we could depend on the promises He made to us. If you put Jesus Christ first in your life and serve Him, He will bless you. You must love Him with all of your heart.

God began to change my life in so many ways. We had about fifteen neighbors whose land bordered our land. One neighbor had fenced about one-half acre of my recently purchased land and would not return it to me, even though I had the surveyor show him it was legally mine. When he took the position that he was not going to permit me to move the fence to the correct location, I decided not to get into a fight with him (I was much larger in stature than he was). In the Bible God says that vengeance is His, so I said, "Lord, I'm turning this over to You." Certain He would take care of it, I got it off of my mind.

Another man was out on my land cutting trees to clear out shooting lanes for deer hunting. When I challenged him, he got belligerent, using dirty language. I simply turned my back to him and walked off, saying, "God here's another one for You to handle."

One wealthy neighbor made an agreement with me. We shook hands, parted company, and he immediately did the opposite of what we agreed. I turned him and that situation over to God as well. I didn't have problems with the other nine neighbors. As a matter of fact, none of them ever contacted me.

The first person I turned over to the Lord had a stroke and could not walk or talk and can't to this day. He was in his mid-fifties. After the disaster struck, his wife told me to put the fence on the line, which I did. The second person was in his upper forties and suffered a heart attack and died. These two disastrous events happened within one to two years after I turned them over to the Lord. If you believe as I do, and if you know God's heart toward people, then you know He wants everyone to repent of their sins and make things right. God is very patient and loves all of us. He doesn't want any of us to perish.

The third man loved money. About five years after

he broke our agreement, he went bankrupt and lost all of his land. For about two months, the property he lost was advertised. It was a ranch of about five thousand acres of land, eight houses, and a lot of equipment. I owned land contiguous with the ranch, along my east property line, and had an interest in owning a 240-acre tract adjacent to my land.

Mitchell, Stacey, and family

I asked my son Mitchell and his wife if they would pay one-third of the purchase price and take title to an eighty-acre tract along the road. They decided that the land along the road was worth more per acre than the other 160 acres with no road access. They would rather buy 100 acres at the ranch's front gate. I didn't say it, but I thought that we probably would not get any land.

My next act in preparing for the land auction was for me to talk to the Lord about us owning it. I went out on the 240-acre parcel and told the Lord that we would love to have it. I said, "God, as You know, I've been reading about You giving the children of Israel the Promised Land. I know it was a beautiful land by the way the Land is described in Your Word. I also know You enjoyed giving it to them and they enjoyed receiving it. God, if You will give this property to my wife and me, I promise that we will enjoy receiving it and owning it." That did not seem like a hard promise to keep.

After I asked God for the land, I felt like I must do my part. What would be my part? I should try to find out what the property would sell for. How do I do that? Perhaps I should ask a qualified profession- al person what they thought the selling price would be. I decided to call the real estate company that was selling the ranch. When I made this call, they connect- ed me with a lady who was a principal owner in the company. I asked what she thought the parcel of land I wanted would sell for. She replied she did not know. I said, "You do this sort of business frequently, and you should be able to estimate a lot closer than I can."

She got a little miffed and replied, "Mister, I don't know what this parcel will sell for."

I said, "Ma'am, I sure wish you would give me your opinion of what you think the amount will be. I must go line up money for the purchase, and I do not know how much to get."

She answered, "Well, you do need to know about what it will sell for, don't you?"

"I replied, "Yes, I do."

She said, "They advertised that piece as good development land. We stated water and electric are on the property and gas is close by. We are expecting it to bring $5,000 to $6,000 per acre."

I said, "Thank you very much."

I did the math and found that they were expecting $1,200,000 to $1,440,000 for the property. I informed June that we needed to go to our bank and inquire about a loan. We met with the bank president and told him what we wanted to do. He asked how much we needed. I simply told him what the realtor said. He knew our banking history and our present economic situation. He said, "We will loan you whatever you need to make this purchase."

When we left the bank I told June, "We will have to decide what debt we are comfortable with. Banks will loan you enough money to get you into trouble." She and I decided we would pay no more than $2,500 an acre for the land.

On auction day we anxiously waited until the parcel we were interested in was offered and were successful at buying the property. We were required to pay 10 percent of the selling price on auction day. The seller had thirty days to provide marketable title, at which time the remainder of the selling price would have to be paid.

My son and his wife got the parcel of land they wanted also. While June and I were waiting for the thirty days to pass, I received a phone call from a national realtor asking if we bought Parcel #9. I said yes, and she asked,

"Do you want to sell it?"

I said, "We don't buy and sell land. We bought it because we wanted it."

She said, "If you were going to sell it, what do you think it would be worth?"

I thought a little bit and remembered the estimated value the lady had told me. "If we were going to sell it, we would probably expect to get $5,000 to $6,000 an acre."

She said, "Well, you didn't pay near that much for it."

I said, "I know, but I didn't think that was the question you asked."

She said, "Well, I'm authorized to offer you five thousand an acre, but if you want six thousand an acre, I'll have to go and get authorization."

She kept my mind so busy, I never thought of the promise I made to the Lord. When June reminded me of my promise to God, I said, "Oh, I never thought of that." The realtor was still on the phone, so I said, "It's not for sale at all." God knew I had not remembered and didn't hold it against me.

Enjoying the land, even in cold Oklahoma weather

After we purchased the land, a man asked if he could work out an agreement to allow him to deer hunt on the property. This relationship grew to be a very close friendship. I soon learned he was my competition in the bidding at the auction. This new friend and I spent a lot of time exploring my land. You know, it's not really mine. It belongs to God. I just get to take care of it for Him, and we all get to enjoy it.

When we purchased this property, I did not realize that this piece of land had so much of my wife's family history tied to it. Her family came to this part of the country soon after 1905. The people were poor, uneducated, hardworking folks. Her family lived in a small town about twenty miles from the land. They would walk over here on Monday morning and work in the virgin hardwood forest with a sawmill crew all week. Then they would walk home for the weekend. Monday morning, they were off to repeat the cycle.

They cut lumber for siding and framing of homes and barns. Hundreds of wagonloads were pulled out of the river delta with teams of horses, and the road used to transport the lumber was located on our recently purchased land. The steel-rimmed wagon wheels were loaded very heavy, and the wheels cut the root systems on all the native plants and trees. The destruction of these root systems caused a lot of erosion, so the roadbeds were about eighteen inches lower than the adjacent soil levels.

I have a front-end loader that I was using to fill in the depressions. June came up to bring me lunch and noticed that I was hauling dirt. She asked what I was doing. I told her I was covering up the depressed roadbeds. She said, "You're covering up my family's history."

I said, "Well, I'll leave a little bit of your family's history, but I'm going to cover up most of the old road-bed."

Over time, we discovered other beautiful features of the land. One morning we got up and were trying to decide what we wanted to do that day. I told June that we owned about sixty acres that we had never seen. "Where is it?" she asked.

"The canyon on the 240 acres. Why don't we get on our four wheelers and ride over to the lower end, then walk up the streambed to the head of the canyon?"

To do this, we rode around the top of the canyon. When we reached the upper end, I stopped my four wheeler and instructed her to get on mine. She wanted to know why, and I told her to trust me. We rode my four wheeler to the lower end and dismounted and walked down into the canyon. The bottom of this canyon had a sandy layer of clean soil, where the water ran when it was rainy weather. This clean, sandy bed of this upland creek is about twelve feet wide. The creek bed meandered back and forth across the bottom of the canyon, which was caused by outer bank erosion.

We trudged up the creek bed for quite a while, and I noticed some wet-looking sand. I pointed it out to June and said I thought a critter could get a drink by digging a little in the wet sand. Because we were in the middle of a very hot, dry, August day, I thought it was unusual for any moisture to be there. We continued on up the creek bed another five hundred feet and discovered a clear pool of water in the creek. It was cold, and I could see small fish swimming in it. It was about fifteen feet across and fifteen inches deep.

We were surprised that the water could remain there at that cool 60-degree temperature. We finally got over the shock of finding the pool and started to walk further up the creek. About five hundred feet further up, there was another pool that looked like it could be a twin to the first one. This one didn't capture us for as long as the first did. Soon we were on our way again, and about another five hundred feet was another pool.

The third pool was different from the other two. Although it was about the same size, the upper side had a sandstone rock formation about thirty feet thick, and a small sheet of water was shooting out from under this huge rock formation, making a beautiful fountain. I concluded that the water was so cold because it came from a source at least thirty feet underground. The water was traveling under the creek bed, and coming through the sand to form the pools. It was a beautiful feature. With some planning, a person could build a unique home around this unusual waterfall.

June said, "Now I know why I never see deer drinking from the hot muddy ponds. They know where the fountain is."

We looked up and were happy to see June's four wheeler sitting there, waiting to take us back to my four wheeler almost a mile away. Now June understood why I wanted her to hop on mine!

We had another great surprise on this land. When June and I were just dating, she had taken me to see a cave with some of the visitors' art on the rocks. It reached about fifty feet into the hillside. The entrance was level and the upper ceiling rock was a couple of feet above our heads. You could walk back into the cave about twenty-five feet. At this point, if you chose to go further into the cave, you had to stoop over to keep from bumping your head. If you were willing to crawl, you might be able to go another thirty to forty feet further. We had owned this new property about a month before we discovered that this same cave was on our land!

One day while walking on the land, I met my wife's uncle. He told me I had bought the Ox Roaster. I asked, "What's the Ox Roaster?" He said that years ago, they used to have cookouts with a large group of Boy Scouts. The landowners at that time built a double-shelf, permanent open fire cooker on a scenic land oversight point. This site also has Indian corn-grinding, ellipse-shaped bowls that were mortar and pestle grinding locations. I loved the area just like the Native people loved it. I felt so blessed and grateful to get to have such a special place, if only for a little while.

There is one more feature I want to talk about that I found on this land. One day I was trimming a place near the upper end of the large canyon, when I discovered a round formation of native stone that a professional mason must have built. When you look at it from the top it looks like a well. It was about three feet wide and only two feet deep. The water in it was cold. I started asking questions about it, because I thought it might be a well that had been filled. I soon learned it was the former owners' drink cooler. They needed cool water for drinks while working in this isolated area.

One of the older men from this area said the former owners were not local residents. He said back in the 1930s and 1940s, they would come out to work on their farm. They would bring one-gallon jars of water, take them down to this spring-fed pool, and submerge them. When they wanted a drink, their water was cool. This made sense to me. There were not any convenience stores, and they were not that mobile. This kind of planning enabled them to get a cool drink of water when they were hot and thirsty.

One day my new deer hunting friend asked, "Did you know that the 160 acres and the big house are for sale?"

I said, "No, I didn't. Why are you telling me about this?"

He said, "Because it's next to the land you just bought."

I said, "Don't you remember? I just purchased a very expensive piece of property. I'm in debt up to my eyeballs on my latest purchase."

He said, "You mean you can't buy this beautiful place?"

I said, "No. What are they asking for it?"

He said, "$1,200,000. It's my life's dream to own a piece of land like the west eighty acres on that place, and if you will buy the east eighty acres and the big house, I'll buy the west eighty acres. You're the only man I know who could afford to purchase it."

My friend didn't have any money, and I didn't have any money. All we had was a desire to own this wonderful property and the courage to try to buy it. We also knew we needed God's help to purchase it. I was older than my friend and had had more time to acquire assets. I thought about what I needed to do to be financially able to purchase the farm and home. I said, "The only way I could buy this property is if I sold some other properties," and I mentioned the properties I had in mind.

His reply was, "I'll help you sell them."

After we sold a couple of these properties, I started negotiations to purchase the 160 acres and home. We were amazed at how it all came about. It was like getting dressed in the morning: Each thing that needed to happen happened at the right time, in the right order. The events necessary to make this acquisition take place could not have been orchestrated more perfectly, and I knew God's hand was in this.

I trusted my friend so much, that I deeded another eighty acres of land to him, so he would be able to borrow his part of the purchase price. It worked like we planned. We soon owned our dream property. He never filed the deed I provided him, and he told me he tore it up. I knew he did just as he said he did. That's the kind of friendship we have.

I turned down the bigger part of a million dollars,

which I could have received by selling the 240 acres of land, and kept my promise to God. I believe that when you honor your promises to the Lord, He will bless you abundantly. I will tell you that I didn't ask the Lord for the second property. I didn't feel like I deserved such treatment, but I did love Him and wanted to please Him in everything I did. Later I was to realize that God was instrumental in us owning both the 240 acres and the big house property. He says He will give you your heart's desires if you make Him first in your life, and He knew my family's history of yearning for land. God understands our love for the land because He created it and put us on it to love it and take care of it. This involves natural blessings as well as spiritual blessings.

To tell you the truth, I am afraid to make a promise to God and not keep it. He hates disobedience, which is sin. He is very patient, compassionate, and forgiving. He will wait on you to turn around and get it right for a long time before He takes His hand of protection off you. Then you're in big trouble! But when you make a promise to God and keep it, or when He asks you to do something and you do it, then the way He blesses you is far beyond anything you could have imagined.

The special home God gave us the opportunity to own.

The special, God-given blessing that I had never imagined was getting the opportunity to own and live in a spectacular home. Still, it is always a walk of faith, every day, and my faith wavers at times. After He made a way for me to purchase these two properties, I started to worry about how I was going to get them paid off. I thought, *I should not be worrying about this. If I really believe God gave me the opportunity to have this land, then He will definitely provide a way to pay for it.* I believe He did just that. It's easy for Him to do. Case closed. I quit worrying, and within three years both notes were paid off. Not only were they paid off, June and I spent a considerable amount of money fixing up our new house.

The architect who designed the house was from Tulsa. When I first bought it, I called him to get a set of drawings and found myself talking to his widow. She was delighted to talk to someone who was interested in her husband's work. She told me the story of how it came about.

A man walked into the architect's office and asked him to design a 16,000-square-foot home. The architect thought he must have meant 1,600-square-foot and asked him to describe the home. The man gave him details of the layout, and the architect thought, *No, he does mean 16,000 square feet!* He asked the man how he was going to pay for this big home, and he told the architect that he had invented a fishing reel, and for each one sold, he received twenty-five cents. He would pay for the house with these quarters. I personally believe that this home was so unique in so many ways, that the inventor of the fishing reel did some of his finest work in designing it.

The big house was built by one of two brothers who manufactured and sold a new type of spinning fishing reel, which was invented by one of them. As plant manager, the younger brother Otto was very much involved in the manufacture of the reels. I'm told he also was involved in their sales. His family loved him very much, and when I bought this property they negotiated an agreement that he would live in another, smaller home on the property until his death. This was fine with me, and I was blessed to get to know him. I sure hated to see him leave when he passed away.

This house is very unique. It's round, and in the style of houses designed by Frank Lloyd Wright. It is a single-level home, with 16,000 square feet of floor space, and there are ten air-conditioners on the roof to cool it. The roof is flat, supported by twenty-eight visible, laminated wood beams. There is a waterfall and swimming pool in the middle of the house, with a skylight dome about twenty-five feet above it. The skylight is also about fourteen feet above the ceiling of the house, and it is twenty-five feet in diameter.

A Plexiglas® wall surrounds the pool for safety and to control the humidity, among other things.

Our home has eleven-foot ceilings in all the rooms surrounding the pool in the middle. There are five bedrooms and seven bathrooms. The house contains eight bedroom-size copper closets, which are round and located 50 percent inside the house and 50 percent outside.

The patio has a built-in charcoal grill with a large vent-a-hood over it. It also has a serving table and four eating tables. We have an indoor patio looking over the pool and waterfall, and enjoy a large, double kitchen.

The hall wraps around the pool and includes a 7-by-65-foot shuffle board of terrazzo flooring surrounded with Mexican tile. (The pucks are about eight inches in diameter.)

There is a large, formal living room that will seat twenty people. One wall has eight, six-by-eight-foot windows, separated by three-foot rock columns, which overlook the lake in the back.

The formal dining room also has large windows, separated by wood columns, so that you can look out over the lake while you eat. The dining room is a twenty-five foot diameter, and approximately one-half of the wall space is glass. The view is stunning.

The beautiful view of the lake that we enjoy from the formal living and dining rooms can also be seen from the breakfast nook. It has a smaller dining table that sits under a chandelier. This house has chandeliers and candelabras all over it. One day I counted the number of light bulbs, and the whole house required about 350! The kitchen has two refrigerators and an ice maker, and we have two other small refrigerators. There is a bedroom located next to the kitchen for a live-in cook/maid.

There is a game room, a large foyer, and a guest receiving room. June and I mostly live in the three-room master suite. It consists of a bedroom with large walk-in closets; an office area with cabinets, desk space, and a morning kitchen; and a sitting room that overlooks the lake.

Adjoining the house is a four-car garage, then there is a swimming pool pump room and two outside utility rooms. These sit just beyond the connected portico. In the back, we have a large, outside patio overlooking the lake, and a 500-foot paved sidewalk with handrails along the edge of the lake. An irrigation building at the water's edge contains a pump to water the lawn with lake water. We also have a two-stall boathouse with a redwood deck. On one peninsula of the lake, there is a small house that was built as servants' quarters. As much as I work around here, I should live there!

As a sharecropper's son, I often feel misplaced in this beautiful home! When we moved into it, my mother told me, "It's exciting now, but it will soon be just your home." If God had not given it to us, I believe she would be right. But when you know it's a gift from God, and I do, it will always be special. I certainly could never have prayed for all this. God knew what He wanted to give to June and me.

CHAPTER 10

A Hobby for the Family

I was working in one of our mobile home parks when my son Mitchell came by and asked if I had seen the beautiful 1933 Chrysler being auctioned off on EBay Motors. I replied, "I haven't looked at it." The next day he again asked if I had looked at the car. I said, "No, I haven't. Son, when I get home I'm too tired to be looking at cars on EBay Motors." The next day Mitchell asked again if I had looked at the car. I said, "No, I did not."

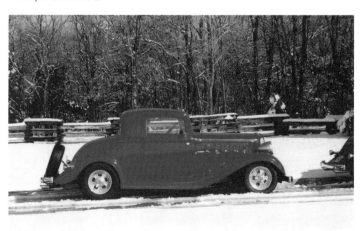

Our first 1933 Chrysler

He said, "I knew you wouldn't, so I printed it off." He asked me to look at it when I got time. When I got home, I took a look at it. I called him and said, "Son, you're right. That's a pretty incredible automobile."

He said, "The auction is already over with."

"How much did it bring?" I asked.

He said, "I don't know." The printing he gave me had the seller's phone number on it, so I called and asked him how much it had sold for. He said that it didn't sell because no one met the reserve. I asked what the reserve was, and he told me.

I said, "I'm working every day except Sunday, so that's the only day I can come to see it. I'm interested, but I'll have to see it and drive it before I will commit to buy it." He agreed to show it to me on Sunday.

June and I drove about five hours to get to the car's location. We looked at it, drove it, and liked it. The only problem was that I'm a tall man, and the steering column did not fit my body. I asked the seller how much it would cost to get a tilt and telescoping column installed and add power steering. He gave me an estimate that was acceptable to me, and I made a deposit on the car. This was my first exposure to the 1933 Chrysler.

This car started me in a completely different direction in my hobby. Since the day Mitchell encouraged me to look at that car, I've been focused on the 1933 Chrysler model only. I like the design work on the body, and I believe the manufacturers did their best cosmetic work in 1933, probably because it was during the Great Depression. Everyone was afraid to spend any money, so automobile manufacturers had to provide something more to get a sale. Staying in business hinged on their ability to bring something special to the marketplace. I have eleven cars built in 1933, nine of which are Chryslers. The other two are a Chevy and a Packard. I like all of them. I would like to have a 1933 Buick, Cadillac, Pontiac, Lincoln, and Studebaker to add to my collection. I guess I'm car crazy!

I've been fortunate to have a brother and sister-in-law who have moved to Oklahoma. When I was at home as a youngster, my brother Steve was fifteen years younger. I was the oldest and he was the youngest, so we didn't get to play together. About five years ago he and his wife Robin started to visit us often. They loved to stay in our unique house, and we loved having them here.

My brother Steve and his wife Robin

The house is located in a rural area, so it is very dark at night, especially when you are in the house. We always put Steve and Robin in the French-decorated bedroom. Steve told me that he got up in the middle of the night and did not believe there was one photon of light in the room to enable him to find the bathroom! He didn't remember where the light switch was, so he felt around until he found his cell phone. He turned it on and used it to light his way. He and Robin were amazed that it was so dark and started to pay attention to where the light switches were.

During one of their visits, I tossed Steve the keys to one of my Chrysler street rods and told him to take Robin for a ride. Afterward, Robin's comment was, "We may want to get one of those." The next time they came, I tossed Steve the keys to another impressive coupe convertible. He took Robin for a ride and she loved it. Her comment this time was, "We will have to have one of those."

1933 Chrysler coupe convertible

I said, "Good luck. I don't believe you will be able

to find one of these to buy." I was thinking of the smaller body styles. I didn't realize they might be interested in an Imperial convertible coupe. The less expensive body is more difficult to find, because these buyers did not have inside storage places and they bought theirs to drive. After Steve and Robin surfed the Internet and saw all the 1933 body styles, they said they would consider an Imperial.

Steve and Robin's 1933 Chrysler Imperial Coupe convertible

I said, "I saw one restored to original condition in *Hemmings Motor News*. You might want to take a look at it. It's high priced, though."

My brother was a very successful man, and when he

wanted something enough, it would fit into his budget. When I showed them the automobile, they bought it and had it shipped to their home in Houston. I suggested he might want to subscribe to the *Hemmings Motor News*, which is where I saw the car. He did exactly that and started watching for a coupe convertible.

One day I was looking through my *Hemmings Motor News* when I noticed a beautiful 1933 Dodge coupe convertible. Just as soon as I saw it, I knew it probably would meet Steve's requirements. I called him and asked, "Did you see the Dodge coupe convertible in *Hemmings Motor News* magazine?"

He said, "What are you trying to pull on me? There is no Dodge coupe convertible in *Hemmings Motor News* magazine."

I replied, "Yes, there is."

He then said, "I have looked thoroughly through the Dodge section, and there is no coupe convertible in this month's magazine."

I then said, "I'll call you back in a few minutes." The car was listed in the street rod section not in the

Dodge section. After I told him the page, he found it.

He said, "We might be interested in it. We'll take a look at it and talk it over and decide if we want it." Shortly, he called me back. "We are struggling with just how to go about seeing it and possibly buying it." I was about three hours driving time from it and had plenty of time to help him, so I drove over and took a look at the car. We had agreed that if I liked the car, I would buy it at a price that I was willing to pay for it; and if he didn't want it for that price, I would keep it for myself. I took a meaningful amount of cash to pay down, in case I reached an agreement with the seller.

Steve and Robin's 1933 Dodge Coupe convertible

When I saw the car and drove it, I liked it and

signed a contract, paying cash to the seller to seal the deal. I should tell you that Steve instructed me not to exceed a certain price if I planned for him to take the car. After I bought the car, I called him and told him I had purchased it for five thousand dollars more than his approved ceiling price. His response was, "Well, I guess I can come up with another five thousand dollars." Actually, I bought it for five thousand dollars less than his ceiling price. I just had to tease him and make him squirm a little before telling him the truth!

The next thing I told him was, "This is more car than what I expected. If you let me drive it to my house and I fall in love with it, it's my car not yours. I think you better come up here and drive it home." I wanted him to look at his purchase, so he would be absolutely sure he wanted it. He and Robin were very excited to own the car. In two days they were at my house with cash in hand to take possession of it. It was very exciting when we went out to get it. The car drove like a dream. We all drove it and raved about its appearance and the workmanship. I don't believe Steve has ever had second thoughts about buying it!

Steve couldn't help but notice the kind of lifestyle June and I live. He and I were raised in this part of the northeast corner of Oklahoma, and he was in his early fifties, considering retirement. I was afraid that he might be too young to be satisfied with only home and family responsibilities. Boy, was my concern misplaced! He adjusted well and quick.

I had a good-sized piece of agricultural land and suggested that he build his retirement home on it. After much thought and exploring all possibilities, Steve and Robin determined they would try to find a place near June and me. I told her, "I will finally have a brother to chum with. He even has an interest in my hobby."

June and I began to look for some property near our place. They wanted to be within a mile or so, and we were soon aware of a place that met almost all of their requirements. The house was small but nice. It was not run down, but it was outdated in architectural style. But it was located on twenty beautiful acres, with a three-acre body of water about fifty feet from the house.

Steve and Robin came up and looked at the property. They decided they liked it and needed to talk to the realtor. They called the agent and set up an appointment with her. I said, "Brother, let me coach you on buying this property." I felt like he was in a unique position to get a very good deal. He was not without skills on making this kind of purchase, but I did have more experience, having purchased fifty pieces of real estate during our marriage.

I told Steve that I thought the land was the bigger part of the value of this place. I said, "Most people who will be interested in this place and have the means to buy it will want more house. That eliminates most buyers that are financially able to purchase it. Tell the realtor you will talk about it and call her back." He did just as I recommended. When he came over to my house, he informed me that he and Robin were interested in the property and wanted to make an offer on it.

I said, "Listen to me, I think you should offer 56 percent of the asking price, and I think you should also tell them you have cash."

He replied, "I'm not going to offer something that low. It will be embarrassing."

June and I were able to purchase our unusual home for about 62 percent of the asking price. I knew he could do the same thing on his buy. I said, "Trust me. You are going to be conditioning them to your way of thinking. You need to establish in the owner's mind that they will probably not get as much as they wanted for this property. It has been on the market the better part of a year. The cost of keeping and maintaining it goes on while they are trying to sell it."

I was able to convince him to make the offer I suggested, saying, "Don't worry. We will up your offer later."

As expected, the realtor responded with a comment like, "I will tell them, but they will reject that low of an offer."

I said to Steve and Robin, "Now you need to be patient and give this situation time to work on the seller's mind." It was difficult, and after waiting about a month and a half, Steve said they didn't want to miss this property. They wanted to raise their offer to 69 percent of the asking price. I said that that sounded okay.

They made the offer and soon got a counter offer asking them to pay 72 percent of the original asking price. Steve informed the realtor that he and his wife would talk it over and he would call her back. He then called me and asked me what I thought. I told him to call the realtor back and ask if the seller was turning his offer down. When my brother asked that question, the realtor's response was, "No, they are not turning your offer down. They will take your offer of 69 percent." He bought the place they wanted at a super price.

Steve and Robin's home

After they sold their Houston home, Steve and Robin proceeded to move into the house they purchased and begin to plan an addition to the home. Once the plans were clearly defined, they asked if they could live in our caretaker's house while the construction was going on. He renamed the caretaker's house the slave's quarters! They stayed there until the house remodel was completed. The outcome of these changes left them with what I'd describe as a luxurious home.

Today Steve and Robin are established in their new home. Like myself, Steve is busy with our hobby. He found a 1933 C. T. Coupe and began rebuilding it into the ride he wanted. The C. T. designation means it was more luxurious than my cars. C. T. cars were originally equipped with an eight-cylinder engine. Most of my cars were equipped with six-cylinder engines. Six-cylinder engine compartments did not require as much room for the engine as eight-cylinder engines did, and this resulted in a longer car.

Steve and Robin's 1933 Chrysler Coupe

Steve decided to put whitewall tires on it, add side mounts, and paint it a different color than what I recommended. I gave him a real nice set of side mount covers. He installed a digital climate control heating and air-conditioning system and a built-in navigation system. When his cars started to outperform my cars at shows, I was soon persuaded to rethink my taste when building a specialty car. I had more cars than he did, but his cars get more recognition when awards are passed out. Since then I've built two more cars, both of which have side mounts.

The Imperial that he bought and a C.T. convertible I recently gave to Mitchell got invited to a concourse show at an elite golf course, and none of mine got invited. Most of our builds have Corvette drive lines in them. They are very roadworthy and are driven to shows within five hundred miles or less from where we live. The Chryslers' hemi engines are too wide to be placed under the hood without altering the hood sides. We simply do not do that. We are completely satisfied with the appearance of these car bodies just as they are.

We ordinarily build what is commonly called a restore rod. I'm doing the opposite on one of my cars the builder is presently working on. Back in 1933, a company stretched these bodies similar to the way we are stretching my car. The company that did this altering was the Lebaron Company. The fact that I'm stretching the hood area allows me to put a Chrysler Viper engine into this street rod. The ten-cylinder engine is long but not very wide. I'm eager to get the stretched car completed.

When I first started to acquire street rods, I was interested in Chevys. My first car after I retired from public work was a 1929 Chevrolet, on which I did most of the building. After I assisted in the rebuild of my first car in high school and then tried it again on this 1929 Chevy, I learned not to do it myself. It takes too long and is very hard work. Probably the reason it took me so long was that I had to do everything two to three times. For instance, I painted it three times. Then I had it painted two more times before I was satisfied.

The next car I had built was an economic disaster.

The builder was a crook and ruthless in his dealings with me. Another builder finally finished it. June and I enjoyed it very much. We drove this car to California to a car show. The car is a pro-street style. It has a Corvette driveline and is super charged. It has a six-speed, standard transmission, is painted Spicy Orange, and has all of the best components. In the end, it cost too much money.

1932 Chevy Coupe we drove to California

When we went to California, the tour was sponsored and led by one of the owners of Vintage air-conditioner company. The show was held at the Pomona fairgrounds and was the 75th anniversary of the 1932 cars. My car was a 1932 Chevy, but the show was featuring the 1932 Ford roadsters. The tour started in San Antonio, Texas, so we took a day to drive there before the tour began. When we arrived at the Vintage Air plant, we saw about fifteen 1932 Ford roadsters, as well as a few other kinds of cars sitting in the parking area. They had the 671 blowers mounted on their engines. All of the roadster owners' exterior performance equipment was visible, because they had no hoods. The occupants of their cars were not protected from the wind or weather.

When June and I pulled into the parking lot, a group of men came to look at our car. Being a bright orange, it stood out. They made sarcastic remarks. One said, "Oh, it's a Chevy." Another said, "Well, I'll tell you one thing, it's orange." This reception did not make me inclined to develop a close friendship with any of these people. I was not mad, but it made me cautious when dealing with them. When we left the gathering, I let those who were listening know my car had something under the hood that was special!

We left the next morning, and I soon decided they did not want to mess with me. I wondered if the blowers were simply cases to look at. Specialty car owners with performance equipment on the engines are usually eager to demonstrate the capability of their cars. I do not know why, but I do know no one wanted to try my car and see what it could do. After I figured this out, I probably shouldn't have, but I taunted them. Like most car owners, I wanted to see how my car's performance would measure up to similar cars. I believe they were afraid of trying to race me, probably wanting to avoid what their buddies would say if they made a run at me and got beat. I never figured out why they could be so testy in the parking lot and not be competitive on the road.

Throughout this whole trip, June and I rode in complete air-conditioned, dry comfort, while the roadster drivers experienced windburn, sunburn, and rain. By the time we arrived in Pomona, they were so red that they looked like beets.

I really enjoyed this trip because we traveled along

Old Route 66. June and I rarely travel on interstates. We prefer other routes, and our favorite is Old Route 66. Running through Oklahoma to points east and west, it is a great way to see our country. It has been my favorite since I was a small boy, when my mother and I took Route 66 to California in our 1934 Ford to see my father, who was in the service there. I even own a short section of it. This historic road also has many wonderful places to see and to stay for the night.

On our road trip to Pomona in our bright orange Chevy, we stopped in Winslow, Arizona. Most of the group stayed in an old railroad station converted into a hotel, called the La Posada Hotel. We had signed up late, so when we asked for a room, they were full. We had to stay in another hotel and were disappointed. I promised June I would bring her back to stay in there someday. Three years later we celebrated our 50th wedding anniversary and spent a night at this special place. We were not disappointed with the facility.

When my brother first joined me showing cars, I told him, "If you get a national trophy with a car, don't expect to win another one with the same car. They only award about twenty-five trophies at the national shows held near us, and two thousand car owners will go home with no trophy at each show." At his first two shows, he brought home a trophy. That just goes to show you I don't know what I'm talking about!

Mitchell took his car to a national show, where there were 2,162 cars registered. I'm told the most cherished trophy awarded at these national shows is to be picked by the National Street Rod Association (NSRA) magazine representative, which publishes reports on these events. A few years earlier I did a photo shoot with another magazine. I wrote a couple of pages containing information on my rod. It was featured on the cover of their magazine, and they did a centerfold article.

When the NSRA photographer picked Mitchell's car, I told him to do a write-up on what led to him acquiring his car. I said, "This write-up should include information on its builder and components. If you do a good job on this write-up, I believe they will feature your car in their national magazine." He and his wife put some time into the report, describing and defining all they knew about his street rod, and I was right. They did a nice three-page article on him and his rod.

My family has gained a lot of coveted awards, plaques, and trophies from the showing of these hobby automobiles. They mean something only to those who do the work or have it done. However, I was taught that whatever you do, do it well. Knowing that you are successful at rising above the normal level is satisfying and fulfilling. We believe that this is honoring the Lord. In whatever we do, it pleases Him when we strive to rise to the best of our ability.

Our car hobby caused me to build a facility on our land to house these high-priced toys. We had a tennis court in our yard, and no one played tennis, so I thought I would use the concrete court for the floor of the new building. It had small cracks, but the surface of the court was level. Then I decided not to use it, because I planned to put tile on the floor, and any movement under it would crack the tile. After pondering what I should do, I decided to use the court as the approach pad in front of the building.

I'm pretty particular about how concrete is formed and reinforced. I leveled the ground behind and adjacent to the court and prepared to install the footings. I borrowed a lazar to enable me to get the concrete as close as possible to being level and square. Our planning included pouring an outside, 20-foot by 84-foot slab on one end. This slab was to serve the shop located at one end of the building.

I poured a driveway with roll curbs from our home's existing concrete to the new building. It was twenty feet wide and ninety feet long. All the concrete was reinforced with one-half-inch re-bars on two-foot centers or closer. After this work was done and the concrete had cured a couple of months, we bought a building and had it erected on the new floor. The rectangular squaring and lazar leveling work paid off. The building turned out perfect.

The erector stated this building was as close as any non-satellite controlled job he had done. The building is 88 feet by 40 feet. It has an eight-foot roof overhang extending the full length of the building. It has six, eight-foot garage doors along the east side, one in each ten-foot section under the overhang. The remaining twenty-eight feet is a shop. The shop is the full width of the building. Our showroom is sixty feet by forty feet. It will hold twelve cars. We decided to cover the floor with quartz tile. It's laid in a black and white, checker-board pattern.

Cushmans, very popular in the 1950s,
adorn our showroom walls.

When I was a young teenager, I wanted a Cushman Eagle motor scooter and a Mustang motor scooter. I decided to adorn the walls with motor scooters. They are placed on mountings on the wall at each end, well above the level of the car roofs, with three on each end in the gable area. I bought a rider for the old-man-type fun. We purchased an old visible gas pump and are shopping for neon signs. At the risk of overdoing it, as most car showrooms are overdone, I'm still adding decorative items. I think I will at least get one neon sign announcing that you are now in the home of 1933 Chryslers. I may get one more neon sign to balance the building décor more than anything else. I haven't decided what I want on it. I think it should say something about the love of God, because He blessed us with this stunning building.

In light of the fact that we have received some attention from people who know a lot about specialty cars, I decided to offer to get a dozen of these 1933 Chryslers to a NSRA show. I proposed that if they wanted to do this at the Midwest Nationals, I would do my part. I requested that they advertise locally and nationally about this portion of their show. They assured me they would comply with the national advertising but had no control over local media.

This is my showroom containing my son's cars, my brother's cars, and my cars. Three of these cars are Chevys, and one is a Chevy pickup. The other two are 1933 Chryslers.

This is the same row of cars looking from the other end.

These family cars are all 1933 Chryslers except one,
which is a 1933 Dodge built by Chrysler.

This is the same row of cars photographed from the other end.

They ran an article calling for all owners of the 1933 Chrysler to bring them to the upcoming event. They announced we would be provided a special parking area. While planning the way this show would be conducted, they wanted me to consent to allowing other brands and other years. I only wanted to participate in the show if it was conducted as I suggested. I felt that if this showing included other kinds of cars and more years, it would dilute the viewing public's focus on these vehicles. I further believe they are so special and rare, that they deserved to have full attention.

The NSRA consented to do it my way. My brother Steve and my son Mitchell took nine of these street rods to the show. They granted my group the privilege of awarding one trophy to the group's selected person. I was hoping that the one selected would be a friend of mine, who has built eight of these 1933 Chrysler street rods. No one in the world has even come close to accomplishing this feat, and I have purchased three of his cars. When the weather turned bad, he left early and didn't get the trophy. However, we were elated that

Mitchell's car was selected instead.

From the first car I helped to fix up, which was my 1951 Ford, I have loved seeing old cars restored to their original glory. I thank God that He gave me and my family the means to have this very rewarding hobby, one that has taken us to so many interesting places and enabled us to meet so many wonderful people.

CHAPTER 11

Seeing the World

After I left my job at the plant and made a good deal of money through my investments, June and I had a lot of time to travel. At first we traveled by car and kind of flew by the seat of our pants. Then we discovered bus trips that enabled us to see things we wouldn't have been aware of had we been in our own car. These trips exposed us to new areas of our beautiful continent of North America.

We traveled to Detroit, Michigan, and headed east, stopping at many attractions. We visited several small towns in Canada, where we stayed at a unique hotel called Chateau Frontenac. In times gone by, this was the hotel of kings and queens. When we got on the elevator to go up to our room, we had an unusual experience. The elevator car was encased in bars and open, so you could see some of the mechanism. This feature alone told me this elevator was very old.

A group of people who had been drinking a lot wanted to get on and squeezed into the elevator. They eventually had so many people that they were unable to close the door, which made them press together even more tightly. Finally the door closed, but the noise the elevator made meant it was very overloaded. It was a little scary and somewhat dangerous, but the elevator did its job and took us to our floor.

This hotel was located on a high peninsula overlooking the St. Lawrence Seaway. It had a large courtyard at the edge of the peninsula, where we could view the beautiful, surrounding terrain. There was a very nice restaurant nearby, which we really enjoyed. The next day we were on our way to Nova Scotia. While we were there, we visited downtown Halifax, using their pedways to see the city. We later went out to Peggy's Cove and ate gingerbread at the lighthouse.

Among the places we went, we saw Franklin Roosevelt's home on Campobello Island, William Vanderbilt's White Castle Mansion, the Biltmore Home, and Thomas Jefferson's Monticello. We also went to

Newport, Rhode Island, and Cape Cod, Massachusetts. Our travels included twelve other bus trips in every direction from our home. There are too many to write about. We have wonderful memories from sightseeing, eating, lodging, and other activities along the way. Each trip left something unique in our minds, and June and I liked some of the places so much, we went back to see them again.

The Biltmore home in Ashville, North Carolina

Our next adventures were cruises in North and Central America. We went up the West Coast to Alaska's coastal cities and took a train to see the interior of the state. We went up the East Coast to Nova Scotia, stopping at various coastal cities. Our memories of these special places are relived many times over. Some people living in the US do not realize that life is altogether different in places very near to them. The services, housing, transportation, diet, and comfort of our neighbors are not like ours.

On a trip to Cozumel, we went with another couple and had nothing special to see or do. We simply wanted to do this trip first class no matter what it cost. When we made our hotel reservations, we asked for the best hotel on the island. When we talked to the hotel, we asked for the best room, which was the penthouse. When we arrived at the hotel, we made reservations at the best restaurant in town. When we ordered our meal, we asked for the best meal they served. Yet, the accommodations were no better than the normal tourist hotel. The food was served on a platter about three feet in diameter, filled with more seafood than we could possibly eat. Although it was beautifully presented, it was gritty and not as good as food served in our hometown. Still, we did enjoy this trip.

We rented a car and drove around town and the island. When we rented this car, the person who delivered it told me not to kill the engine. He instructed me to let it run all day, which I did. While I was driving in an undeveloped area, we saw indigenous wildlife. The wildlife had some similarities in appearance to our local animals, but none looked like ours. We thought one looked like a raccoon. The next one resembled an opossum.

As we progressed around the island, we found an area where iguanas were present. One ran out in front of the car, and I could not avoid hitting it. It made a loud noise, and I got out of the car, expecting to find a dead iguana. There was no body or blood. I inspected the car and found a dent in a door. I concluded that he somehow avoided the wheel and was able to strike the door with his tail, leaving him unscathed. When the day's travel was over, I took the car down and filled the fuel tank up. Gasoline cost eleven cents per gallon! When we were through traveling for the day, I turned off the engine.

We entered the hotel dining room to eat and were surprised that only one other couple was there. The waiter was constantly at our table, trying to be of assistance to us. The band was playing music, and in their broken English, they asked if we had requests. We knew none of their Spanish songs, and getting too much attention made us feel uncomfortable. After eating, we went to our room, and I wandered out on the private balcony. While I was looking out over the beach and ocean, I saw a couple in the water. They were bobbing up and down vigorously, as though they were bobbing for apples. They sure were having a good time.

Later I stood on the balcony, just looking around and enjoying the peace and solitude of the evening, when I saw what I thought were rats running around on the beach. The penthouse was so high, I could not determine what was happening, so I decided to go down and find out just what was going on. The rats were actually crabs, and there were many of them.

The next day the rental car would not start. We

called the rental company, and a man arrived to start it. He loosened the distributor and advanced the timing, then he put it into the running position. The engine was so worn out, it must never start without advancing the spark. He instructed us to leave it running all day.

We went to Chankanaab Lagoon and did some snorkeling. The water was unbelievably clear. I think I could clearly see a fourth of a mile under water. The fish were stunningly colorful, and there were so many varieties. The coral was abundant and beautiful. At every stop that day, even while snorkeling and shopping, we left the car running and no one bothered it. This trip was entertaining!

My wife and I traveled to Hawaii along with her brother and his wife. My sister-in-law had worked hard to plan the trip, reserving timeshare condominiums as housing. Some were located on beaches and others were inland. I learned that the roar of the ocean waves crashing against the shore are not as soothing as some say. If you are not used to the sound, it keeps you awake.

The four islands we visited were all a little different, with unique sites that we found enjoyable. On one of the islands, we stayed in a condominium located inside a coconut grove. The trees were very tall, and most had coconuts on them. I found four or five coconuts lying on the ground and picked them up. Back in our kitchen, eventually I opened up one for our consumption. It was good!

Early in our marriage, June had had a job as a rural mail carrier and had seen coconuts mailed to others. The post office accepted them with the address printed on the coconut shell with a magic marker. We decided to mail a few to folks at home this way. The postage was a lot more than the coconuts cost in local markets. This was not something you would choose to do to save money. It was fun to surprise the recipient with a peculiar gift.

While we were there, I found a very short tree in the grove. We had an old VCR recorder, so I walked under it and shot some pictures of the coconuts on this twelve-foot high tree. After I shot the pictures, I was careful not to show anything that reflected the fact the tree was short. Then I went up to the outside balcony and yelled down to June's brother to catch the camera, indicating I was going to toss it down to him. When the women watched the daily recordings, my wife and sister-in-law were convinced I had climbed one of those tall trees to photograph the coconuts. I also had a lot of fun with others later as the recording was watched.

On all the islands, we rented cars to go to all the tourist sites. We went to the isolated areas and missed little. We attended a luau, and I was drafted to demonstrate how to do a Hawaiian dance. I saw it on tape and thought I was a real showman. Truthfully, it was awful!

When our children were young, June and I took them on a vacation to Canyon City, just south of Amarillo, Texas. They have a very good museum, which we enjoyed much more than our children did. We went there to see the show, Texas in Palo Duro Canyon, which all of us enjoyed. The climate in this area is dry, and the show is written to bring out the fact that folks who live there always have been and are constantly yearning for rain. They tell how desperate people are for it, and when it does rain they become extremely excited. After many pitiful accounts of just how bad the drought was, the people are elated at the visual signs of an approaching rainstorm, the answer to their prayers.

Mitchell, Lisa, and me in 1968 at Palo Duro Canyon

The show is staged in a canyon with a large, round rim. As the drama builds, there is lightning and thunder (provided by detonating primer cord along the canyon rim). Then, just as the play made it look like it was storming, it really did rain. The cast was so amused, they started laughing as big raindrops hit them. My family will always remember the perfect timing of the storm.

In the afternoon our children wanted to go swimming in the motel swimming pool. This pool was kidney shaped and looked like a child's wading pool. It was small and didn't look like it was very deep. Sometimes looks are deceiving, especially to small swimmers. Our six-year-old son Mitchell jumped in and disappeared under the water. When his feet finally hit the bottom, he reached up for something to hold onto. I quickly knelt down, reached out as far as I could without falling into the pool, grabbed his hands, and lifted him to the top of the water. He was coughing and frightened, but soon he wanted to try the pool again. This time he was careful to stay in the shallow end. The children had a good time playing in the pool, and I learned it is necessary to watch your kids at all times!

On another trip we went to Farmington, New Mexico, and rented a room in a comfortable motel. Our plan was to drive to the many ancient Anasazi and Aztec Indian ruins. We decided to go to the Aztec National Park located in Aztec, New Mexico. The park contains examples of the housing used by the Aztec people in the 1200s. The rebuilt great kiva, which is a room used for religious rituals, is impressive and interesting to see. We went to the impressively large ruins at Chaco Canyon. It is thought to have had a population of about five thousand people at the peak of its occupation, but at some point the people disappeared. There is speculation on why they left, but no one really knows. They built many interesting buildings, roads, and structures, such as water control devices.

We also saw Mesa Verde National Park. It is located west of Durango, Colorado, on a very large mesa or plateau. Our park service has preserved several locations, where the Anasazi Indian Nation lived several hundred years ago. The ruins are mainly remains of their houses and irrigation systems, which enabled them to use the available moisture for farming in this very arid land.

The most notable of these ruins is Cliff Palace. The

day we were there was a very cool day, late in the fall. The site contained ladders leading down to a site where overhanging rock structures protected the occupants from the weather. The ruins contain approximately one hundred dwellings and storage bins for their grain. There were site guides present to help you understand how they lived.

As we were absorbing all the information being shared by the park's guides, I noticed the weather was changing. Then I noticed a few snowflakes falling. The moisture was not falling on us, because we were under this massive rock overhang. The location was selected by the former colony of occupants because of this natural shelter. While I was walking around imagining their way of life, I noticed the snow was accumulating on the sagebrush, and the flakes were getting larger and more plentiful. I was not worried, because I was driving a large Chrysler with a positive traction differential and snow tires. Even so, in a few minutes I suggested that we go to our car and start our journey out of the park.

When we reached our car, it had a quarter inch of

snow on it. We were twenty miles from the highway, and as we drove out of the park, the snow got deeper. Our progress got slower as the snow got deeper. Then the snow tires began to spin. This was frightening because there were no guardrails on the road, which had a perilous drop on our side. When both rear wheels spun because of the positive slip feature, the car slid off the road. Only the grass at the edge stopped us from going over the edge. June screamed, and this happened three times.

I decided to risk driving on the other side of the road. Being in the wrong lane, I knew we could meet another car head-on, but I also knew that the snow was probably keeping people from coming up to the top of the mesa. By this time, the snow was about eight inches deep. The ditch along the "wrong" side of the road had a deep, curved concrete invert. This curvature allowed the edges of my snow tires to make contact with the concrete, and the added friction allowed us to continue moving.

The ice-coated grass and sagebrush were rubbing heavily against the side of the car. I visualized losing all of the paint on that side, but I didn't care. Getting out safely would be well worth the cost of a paint job. We did meet an oncoming rescue vehicle, but it was traveling very slowly. They stopped and asked questions about the number of people stranded in the park. They told us to continue doing just what we were doing and instructed us not to get out of the car if we had to stop. They said they would not leave without rescuing us. Even though we had this life-threatening experience, we still hold the Mesa Verde visit as being very special.

The Rocky Mountains and Southwest Desert are beautiful. We have visited numerous tourist sites, including Bandelier National Monument, Canyonlands National Park, Canyon de Chelly National Monument, and Box Canyon Falls, to name a few. All these sites were a good entertainment experience.

We have taken three cruises that were notable. One of them started in Los Angeles, California. Our travel group consisted of June and me, her cousin Joyce, and her husband Jerry. They are our traveling buddies on most trips. Jerry and I have been good friends from a young age, and I knew him long before I knew June. While we were lined up to board the ship, we discovered we were behind a nice couple from Australia. Their names were Barry and Carol. I'm very talkative and soon struck up a conversation with them. They were also blessed with a gift of gab, and we enjoyed the whole cruise with them.

Seated: Bill York, Joyce Lepper, Jerry Lepper
Standing: June York, Ronald McMillan, Evelyn McMillian,
Carol Todd, Barry Swanbrough

After we boarded, we sailed south along the Mexican Riviera, visiting the coastal cities with our new friends. We dined and attended shows, and we all enjoyed each other. We shared things about our lives, and we found our differences and similarities very interesting. We were from a rural area in the central part of the United States, while they were from a coastal city of Australia. Our lifestyles were very different. They were apparently much better off financially than we were. I find it better to let people believe we are not as well off as we really are. When the truth is known, it is easier this way. We were impressed that although they thought we were poorer than they were, they were happy to become our friends.

Barry and Carol, friends from Australia

While visiting with them, we found out they often visited the large cities in the US. We encouraged them to visit the inner rural areas, and I invited them to come to our house and stay. Then we could take them by car to tourist sites nearby. I did not tell them anything about our house. I only told them we had purchased an old house and were fixing it up. They promised they would take us up on our offer, and within a few months they contacted us and asked if the offer still stood. We said, "Yes, we are looking forward to your visit." We agreed to meet them at the airport and drive them to our home.

Joyce and Jerry Lepper

The evening they arrived, Jerry, Joyce, June, and I met them and decided to go get something to eat before traveling to our house. This meant that we didn't get home until after dark, so we asked Jerry and Joyce to spend the night also. When we first arrived, and our Australian friends saw our home, they could not believe their eyes. They were stunned! We put them in the French bedroom and went on to the living room, while they were getting settled. Soon they came out of their room, ready to see the rest of the house.

As we were walking, I discovered a pair of my old tennis shoes sitting in the hall and picked them up. Barry said, "Them are me shoes."

I asked, "Why are they in the hall?"

He said, "Me left them in the hall so me can find me room."

Laughing, I put them back down. Being round, there are no reference points in the house. I understood his problem.

These people were easy and pleasant to be around. They seemed to be comfortable with who they were, needing to impress no one. They talked a little different but were easy to understand. What they said was exactly what they meant. They were clean, generous, soft spoken, loving, caring people. We showed them the heartland of our country, and they invited us to visit them in their lavish home, which sits on ocean frontage in a small town near Sidney, Australia. Because I have claustrophobic tendencies, the eighteen-hour flight has prevented us from doing that, but we enjoyed every minute of the time they were here.

On another trip Jerry, Joyce, June, and I went to Cancun on a plane. This was my first time to see a very different way of life. At this time, there were few tourist facilities in Cancun, and we were booked into the Calinda Hotel for about a week. When we arrived, we were tired from traveling all day, so we decided to take a refreshing shower. I got in the shower first and stepped back when I turned on the water, not knowing how cold or hot it would be. To my surprise, it was rust-colored and did not change for a long time. It finally got fairly clear and a little bit warm. I wondered if I was the first person to use the shower after construction, because it looked brand new. If it was new, it must have been plumbed with used pipe.

After we showered, we decided to go downtown and see the city. The four of us got into a cab and asked about a ride to town. The driver informed us the fare would be $.80 to go anywhere in town. That fare paid for all four of us! Our food and other purchases were also very inexpensive, and everywhere we went, the people tried to get us to spend our money with them. The hotel informed us that tour guides were available to advise us on various things to do and see. They seemed to be a little inexperienced in their presentation. All of the recommended activities were tailored to keep you among the other tourists. We wanted to see how the residents lived.

We were invited to go on a glass-bottom boat ride to see the sea life. The guide described the beautifully colored fish and other sea life in these waters. This presentation made the four of us want to see the beauty of the sea. We made several trips to various parts of the city. On one of these trips, we asked the cab driver how we could see how the residents live. He advised us to take a local ferry to the Isla Mujeres.

The ferry, loaded with local residents, took us about three miles across a body of water to the island. All of us had to stand up the entire trip. I was not in the least uncomfortable with the local people. They let all of us have positions along the edge of the boat, so we could see the beautiful fish. This trip cost us $.35 each. None of us spoke Spanish, so we couldn't talk to anyone. All we could do was smile, and there were lots of smiles on the whole trip.

When we got to the island, there were no taxicabs. They had small motorcycles for rent, so we rented two of them, one for each couple. I was thirsty and knew not to drink the water, so we stopped at a local bar. When you don't drink, a small amount of alcohol has a big effect on your ability to do normal things. Their drinks are mixed with a lot of tequila, so drinking there affected me in a big way. I could barely walk, and June was very brave to trust me on that motorcycle! But no one got hurt, and we all had a good time. When we boarded the ferry to go back to the mainland, the fare was $.40 each. I never understood why it cost more for us to return to the mainland.

The next day we signed up to go on an inland trip to see the Mayan ruins at Chichen Itza. The trip included traveling about a hundred miles by bus on narrow roads. The villages we passed through were occupied by residents, who had nothing except what they could get out of this tropical jungle. Most of their houses were one room, with hammocks visible inside them. I came to the conclusion that there must be a lot of snakes in the jungle, and the hammocks helped protect them while sleeping.

The walls of their homes were constructed of small trees, about three inches in diameter, vertical poles lashed together with bark. Doors and windows were just openings. I would expect the weather was so hot, they probably slept cooler this way. There was evidence that the Peace Corp was helping them. They had built ten-foot towers with open containers on top and pipes running into their houses. There were ladders leaning on the concrete structures to enable them to climb up and pour water into the containers. The system allowed them to have showers.

In one village I saw a slim hog tied up with a rope around his neck. That would be impossible to do with hogs here, because their necks are larger than their heads. While we were traveling on the bus, we saw a man standing beside the road with a high stack of hats in his arms. We stopped, and he boarded the bus, saying, "At Chichen Itza, it will be very hot and sunny, and you will need to buy one of these hats." The hats were inexpensive, and I believe all the passengers bought one.

When we arrived, a young man started to follow me around, trying to sell a quartz statue to me. I tried to get him to reduce his price, but he left me and went on to someone else. I intended to buy his statue and felt bad when I could not find him later. The price of the small statue meant almost nothing to me. I was just having fun. But to him it may have meant the difference between going hungry or not. It made me feel bad when I couldn't find him.

We also traveled to Tulum Ruins, which is located about twenty miles south of Cancun and is on the coast. This is a Mayan temple. When we arrived there, I immediately went to a concession stand to purchase some of the favorite local food, which is something I always do. As I ate what they called a taco, I commented on how good it tasted. A local lady, who was fluent in English, said, "You like our food, do you?"

I said, "Yes, I do."

She said, "You know why it tasted so good, don't you?"

I replied, "No, I don't."

She said, "Look up." I looked up and didn't see anything. She then said, "You do not see any electric wires do you? The chicken was alive and the vegetables were in the garden this morning. The freshness was what made it taste so good." I wonder if we Americans are not being shortchanged in some ways and we don't realize it. The Tulum Ruins had guides to tell us the history of the previous occupants, and we enjoyed learning about them.

A trip we made with my wife's family included her brothers Ronald and Jim and their wives Evelyn and

Rita. We boarded a ship in San Diego and traveled down the west coast, visiting the coastal cities of Mexico and Central America. We stopped at Puerto Vallarta and took a bus ride to a small town called Zihuatanejo. When we arrived, we again wanted to see the local residents' way of life. We found it to be a clean town. No one had trash around their homes, and they left their doors open. I think they wanted us to see inside their homes.

One lady invited us in. Her home was only three rooms: a bedroom, a dining room, and a living room. All the rooms were about ten foot by ten foot in size. She cooked in her yard, in a clay, beehive-type oven. We found we understood her broken English, and she told us that the large rocks in her backyard were their clothes dryer. They simply spread their clothes on the sun-heated rocks to dry. They had chickens in the back yard for eggs and meat.

When our tour of the woman's house was over, I tipped her five dollars, which earned me a big smile. I felt I got my money's worth! They probably had dairy cows or goats for milk, and we had seen large gardens along a creek as we entered their town. The people had things to sell. Imports were expensive, but anything they made or cooked locally was not.

The next stop was Acapulco. This city is set up to please the American traveler and get as much of your money as you would part with. We visited lavish homes on mountainsides with wonderful ocean views. The hotel we visited was beautiful, but we stayed on the ship, so we only saw the lobby and pool. The large pool had a bar next to it, with the bar stools in the pool. The most memorable event we saw there were the cliff divers. We had seen this on television, but it looks more frightening in person!

When we got to Costa Rica, we took a bus into the mountains. The roads were hard surfaced but very narrow. The coffee fields were pretty, with their colorful brown and red beans. I saw no one working, probably because it was a weekend. The houses were small, three or four rooms for the average resident. They talked about the cost of living being very reasonable and told us that the average electric bill was twelve dollars a month.

If we lived like they live, our cost of living would be something to talk about too. I looked inside several of their homes and saw only one small light bulb hanging from the center of the room. They had a small refrigerator and a small, portable television. On Sunday everyone went to church and then took a walk. I was amazed at how many people were walking down the roads.

Most people made their living from the coffee business, and a few made their living from the tourists. I saw very few automobiles and no emergency vehicles or police officers. I didn't think they had any crime, because they have nothing to steal. If you are looking for a place without stress, this might be a good place to live, but the lack of entertainment might be boring.

As an engineer, going through the Panama Canal was fascinating. I appreciated the multiple challenges of building and operating it. It was built in the early 1900s, and the mechanisms were outdated but still worked. I loved watching the locomotive operators cooperating with the ship's crew as the large vessels moved through the locks. The inland waterway through Panama is a very pretty place, especially Gatun Lake. It takes a tremendous amount of water for each ship to go through the canal, and it operates twenty-four hours a day, moving seafaring vessels from the Pacific Ocean to the Atlantic Ocean or vice versa.

After we were through the canal and into the Atlantic, we stopped in Cartagena, Columbia. Like all large cities, it has both poor and rich housing districts. They naturally wanted to show us the best part of their city, so we went to the large, expensive homes. However, we also saw the inexpensive housing. I noticed that all the wealthy homes had bars on every door and window, and most of their best homes were not as impressive as our average homes.

We saw horses and wagons traveling with the motorized vehicles. These horses were running very fast to keep up with cars. I believe they must do this every day, because they were so thin. They must run for miles and miles. The day we were there, I saw a woman riding a small motor scooter in the city traffic. She was all dressed up, but she was moving in and out through traffic at a fast speed, like she did this every day. The automobiles were poorer in quality, and the office buildings were not equal to what you see here at home, but it was a very enjoyable day.

Some places we went to did not leave much to talk about, but this event happened in Kingston, Jamaica, and it was not pleasant. In America, we eat good, clean food for the most part, and the general public doesn't see how that food, especially meat, comes to the table. In Jamaica, we saw a pickup truck with two dead, gutted steers in the back. As they were hauling them down the road, blood and dust were all over and the carcasses were bouncing around. I wondered what we might be exposing ourselves to when eating outside the US, where there was no Food and Drug Administration to regulate what we put in our bodies. Still, overall our stop in Jamaica was enjoyable.

I usually try to buy June a piece of jewelry on each of

our trips, and we walked all over the tourist section of Kingston, looking for a memorable piece. On our way back to the ship, a very small, old lady began following us, strumming a little guitar. I treat people with respect, especially if they are older than I am. So I stopped and listened to her sing and play, but it was not sounding very good. Three old men sat on a bench, pointing and snickering, so I clapped when she finished. This was back in the 1980s, when dollars were prized possessions, so I got out my billfold and gave her a five-dollar bill. When the old men saw how much she earned, their mouths fell open. I hope they didn't take it away from her!

On one of our trips we went to Aruba, but this trip left me with only a few memories. Aruba is a small island in the South Caribbean Sea, and we traveled there by ship for only one day. We went on a shore excursion, which included a tour around the island. It was uncomfortable because women cleaned the restrooms while we used them. I was not used to that kind of a situation! However, I didn't notice any of them paying any attention to me.

We stopped for about an hour at a very large rock formation, giving us plenty of time to climb it for a better view of other parts of the island. The site was equipped with handrails and cleared walkways. Near the bottom of the descending path, however, there was a large rock across it, with a three-foot tall opening we had to pass through to proceed down the path. It was very steep at this point. Most people had some difficulty maneuvering through the opening. My wife was one of the people behind me when I passed through the obstacle. I helped her and another lady get through. Since the bus was not scheduled to leave for several minutes, I stayed to help others get through. One of the people I helped was a young teenage girl. When she wiggled though the opening, her skirt slid up and I could not believe what I saw. She had no panties on! I decided it may not be a good idea for me to help any more.

Another of our cruises started in Vancouver, Canada, and moved into the Pacific Ocean, about where the tongue of Alaska starts. This trip included a visit to Sitka, Alaska, which is a small town on the west side of Baranof Island. The town was established by fur traders and is not densely populated. There are a lot of fur trader villages in this area of the country.

We were ultimately going to the Hubbard Glacier, and our traveling party included June and me, Steve and Robin, and my sister Treva and her husband Mark. We had visited several other glaciers on other trips to Alaska, but none were like the Hubbard Glacier. My brother is a world traveler and for many years traveled on business to desolate places, helping an oil company make investments in oil reserves. These reserves are located all over the globe in mostly undeveloped locations. He told me that in all his travels, the Hubbard Glacier was the most impressive.

The glacier was about two miles wide and about forty feet high. The cruise ship traveled very close to it, and it moved at an unusually fast pace. The movement caused the glacier to calve, which is when pieces break off, frequently. When this occurred, the sound produced by a mile of forty-foot thick ice breaking was huge. The activity of Hubbard Glacier caused the protected bay to be loaded with large icebergs, but our ship simply pushed them out of its way. It turned in a circle to allow everyone on board to see the phenomenal glacier. This trip was well worth our time and money!

All of these trips, shared with friends and family, are just another example of how the Lord will bless you with something you could never have imagined. Seeing all these places and their natural wonders makes you more certain that our Almighty God is truly the Creator of them.

CHAPTER 12

Our Spiritual Life

Now June and I are older, have had some success in the business world, and feel good about who we are. We know we owe everything to God and feel blessed in so many ways, but then after you have pushed yourself to obtain your goals in life, you should carefully evaluate the importance of all your future moves. I've seen people who are always hungry for more financially, no matter how much they have. Some are still piling up wealth in the last days of their lives. Many times only the government and the lawyers are rewarded when they pass away.

A few years ago I announced to June that I was no longer going to try to make any additional money through investments, because I believed we had enough to sustain us to our deaths and leave to our children. There are times when situations and opportunities arise, and I know I could make more money, but why should I attempt to earn what I don't need? You may say, "Earn it for your heirs." I believe they either have the ability to earn and the wisdom to take care of their earnings or they don't. If they do, they don't need my money; if they don't, I couldn't give them enough to sustain them and would give them no incentive to do better on their own.

When you get to the last years of your life, you think about these things. If you look up the word "inheritance" in the Bible, you will see that it is a major issue with God. He says that it's a blessing for parents to leave an inheritance for their children and their children's children, and especially to leave them land. That's something June and I have done for our children, and it blesses us to be able to bless them in this way.

When you are a Christian, God lives in your heart. You take Him with you wherever you go, and He helps you to do your best to deal with all the circumstances you encounter. You endeavor to obey His instructions in all that you do. Throughout the Bible, God made it clear we are to deal with people fairly and honestly. In our family life and in doing business, He teaches us to always be fair with others. June and I have tried to do this throughout our married life. In our business, I tell people who work for us that if anyone gets short-changed or cheated, make sure it's me who gets the short end of the stick.

As a Christian, you are always thinking about ways to live your life better. To me, that means not only pleasing God but also pleasing others whenever you can. I was told a man I know had only gone to church with his wife one time during their thirty-five years of marriage. She suddenly died and left him alone. Later, I was told that he has only missed church once since her death. This got me to thinking: Do we need to do some soul-searching to see if we have our priorities in order?

I really don't believe that a lot of people who profess to be Christians are enjoying all of what God has available for them. To please God, we must be humble and serious in our endeavor to serve Him. If we do not read His Word and search our souls to make sure we are thinking, speaking, and acting right, we will not receive all the blessings He has for us. He wants us to have the full measure of His spiritual and material blessings.

Recently, we had a situation that illustrated this to me. Our large home is electrically powered, but I discovered that our property had natural gas deposits. It is much less expensive to heat a home with natural gas, so I checked my title records and found that I owned 50 percent of the mineral rights on my property. The other 50 percent was owned by a Christian-affiliated organization. I called their representative to see about using some of the gas we jointly owned. I asked what they might expect in return or if I could buy their share of the mineral rights. They said they had a policy of never selling mineral rights, and if I wanted to use any of the gas, I must pay them for 50 percent of the quantity used at current market price. If I sold any gas from under my land, they expected 50 percent of the money.

I asked, "How can we go about sharing the cost of developing these reserves fairly? To develop the gas field would require a lot of my time and money. It's only fair for you to pay me for half of the hours

I invest in the development." They informed me that they would not pay for half of my labor or any other cost incurred in the development process.

I decided to meet with them in person. When I did, I told them, "You are clearly not dealing with me honestly and fairly. We own this asset equally, and so the profits and the costs should be shared equally." This is the way I believe Christians should do business, and if everyone in our country did business this way, we would live in a much more prosperous and joyful world.

Unfortunately, I believe we have lost the values of my generation and previous generations, who were mostly Christians. Even many who didn't go to church still lived according to Christian principles, because our nation was founded on them.

Consider the work ethic that has been nearly lost. A friend of mine told me that in the thirties, when the oil fields were being developed in Oklahoma, a man he knew got a job as a roughneck working for a fledgling oil company. This man had a house full of children, and roughneck wages were very low. He was having a hard time, so he asked the company owner for a pay raise. The owner asked him what he was willing to do to earn more money. The man said, "Well, I already work very hard for you, but I guess I could work seven days a week to earn more money." They agreed to this, but after a few weeks it became apparent that his earnings still were not enough to support his family.

The man again went to his boss. Again, the boss asked him what he had in mind to enable him to be worth more money. He said, "I have been thinking about that, and I'm willing to work from daylight to dark to earn the needed money for my family." The boss agreed, but the man continued to struggle to provide for his family. The man saw no other option but to tell his boss that his earnings were still not enough to meet his family's needs.

As expected, his boss said, "How can you increase your value to me?"

He told the boss, "I knew you would ask this question, and I cannot work any more hours, because the oil patch is too dark and dangerous at night. I'm already working as hard as I can. The only thing I can think of that would be beneficial to you is for me not to walk anywhere. When I need a tool, I'll run to get it."

Today, I don't know of anyone who would go to such lengths to earn a raise in pay. This worker had a solid work ethic that you should earn your living; you don't expect it to be given to you. Life was a lot tougher back then, but people had good values and morals. Today too many people think they should get what they want without earning it. This attitude of expecting free food and housing is a common way of thinking, but it's wrong, and it will get you nowhere in life. The roughneck worker I'm writing about eventually was promoted to be vice president of the oil company!

A man I worked with told me this story about when he was a boy. His dad worked in the Oklahoma oil fields near Oilton. His father also had low earnings and a large family, some of which required medication and doctor treatment frequently. The doctor would treat the family's ailments and write down the amount of the cost in a book, keeping track of each family's debt.

The family was paying all they could each month on the debt, but it was not getting smaller.

His father approached the doctor about the possibility of him and his boys working to pay the debt. The doctor said, "I've recently purchased some land and need the fence right-of-way cleaned out and a fence built." My friend said the land had continuous scrub brush oak trees all along the fence line. The project took several weeks during the summer, when the weather was brutally hot and the days were long. On the days they could work, they had to carry their drinks and lunch. They took several gallon jugs of water wrapped in burlap cloth, because if they kept them wet, they would stay cool enough to be drinkable. Their lunch consisted of tomatoes, because they had had a large crop of them.

One day my friend broke out in a rash all over his body. He said he itched so much, he was unable to scratch enough. His dad said, "Well, son, I'm trying to lower my doctor bill, but I guess I'll have to take you to him."

The doctor asked my friend, "What have you been

eating? "My friend told him about eating tomatoes for his lunch every day. The doctor said, "Young man, you have overloaded your system with acid. Stop eating those tomatoes."

My friend said, "I thought it was hard to work hard all day building fence with only tomatoes to eat, but I soon learned it was even harder to build fence and then watch my brothers eat tomatoes while I could only drink water."

My Grandpa York was one of the people who worked in the oil fields of Oklahoma. He was working on an oil well drilling machine while it was in operation. His job was oiling the equipment while it was drilling. The oil field was very dangerous, as the open gears were everywhere. While trying to oil the gears, a string hanging from his tattered jacket got caught in one of them as it turned quickly. It pulled his arm through the set of gears and cut off his arm. At the time this happened, he had a house full of children. After this tragedy, it was tough for the family to survive, but they never stopped working to support themselves.

Where does this work ethic come from? I believe it comes from our God, who worked on Earth for six days and rested on the seventh day. This project of developing, shaping, and filling the Earth with both plant and animal life was a great task, and when we read through those first two chapters of Genesis, we see that God always does things the right way and in the right order. Everything He does is *good*. For example, in Exodus, when Moses led the children of Israel out of Egypt, they wandered in the wilderness for forty years, and yet their clothes and shoes never wore out. This was a miracle that God did because there were no materials in the wilderness to replace them. He took care of them when they couldn't take care of themselves. He loved them that much.

The most important issue about material wealth is that we must be sure it doesn't own us. The Bible says it is the love of money that is the root of all evil not money itself. It's important to make our spiritual treasure the real wealth in our lives, to love the Lord more than anyone or anything else. When your life is over and your judgment day arrives, I believe you will face Him to give an accounting for your life.

If you are not prepared to meet Him, you will be extremely frightened and absolutely helpless at your death and the day of your judgment. You must ask God to forgive you for all your sins and surrender your life to Him now, because this opportunity only exists while you are alive on Earth. After death, it is too late. You lose this precious chance for redemption.

Before I go any further, I want to talk a little about sin, because many people misunderstand the meaning of it. What is sin? In the Bible sin is simply disobeying the guidelines and laws that Almighty God, who is perfect, set in place for us to live by and please Him. All people have sinned. You know exactly what I'm talking about. When you sinned, you felt guilt and shame and suffered the consequences for disobeying God. And you may feel trapped in some of your sins. You believe you can control yourself, but then you continue making the same mistakes over and over. God gave us all the choice to obey Him or disobey Him.

The Bible helps us understand sin even more by naming them. And Jesus made it clear that habitually *thinking* on sin is the same as actually *committing* the sin. Some of those mentioned are: sexual immorality, idolatry (this is worshiping anything or anyone other than the God of the Bible), witchcraft, jealousy, fits of rage, murder, lying, breaking your word, gossip, and especially pride. If you consider all the sins listed in the Bible, you come down to one common denominator: selfishness and self-centeredness.

Jesus was totally unselfish and never self-centered. He laid down His life for all of your sins by dying for you on the Cross. It was His innocent blood that paid your debt to God for your sin. Then He was raised from the dead to prove that He was the sinless One, who qualified to pay the price for mankind's sin. And right now, Jesus is asking you to surrender your life to Him. He's saying that He loved you so much that He died for you. He did this so you could be forgiven of all your sins — past, present, and future — and have a brand-new life as God's child, restored to the Father.

Today is the time to act. I urge you to receive Jesus as your Lord and Savior now. Again, after death it is too late. Your spirit and soul will leave your body forever. Did you know that you are a spirit with a soul (mind, emotions, will) that lives in a physical body? When your physical body gives out on you, your spirit and soul will leave your body and the condition of your spirit will determine whether or not you go to Heaven.

Our spirits are separated from God, and only surrendering our lives to Jesus changes that. If we give our lives to Jesus, the Holy Spirit makes our spirits brand-new. He restores us and joins our spirits to the Father. After we do this, the Holy Spirit gives us His strength to stop sinning and to say no to the sins we used to commit.

Becoming a child of God through Jesus Christ is a choice only you can make. Nobody can make it for you or force you to do it, because it is a change in your heart. Many people let the wrong behavior or teachings of some Christians stop them from coming to Jesus. Don't let those who are wrong in some way stop you from receiving the greatest gift God gave to mankind! Take a good look at Jesus in the Bible and decide for yourself.

If you make the choice to receive Jesus as your Lord and Savior, then you will not be afraid when you die. You will know you are going to Heaven. The Bible says that when you are absent from the body, you will be present with the Lord.

If you would like to do this right now, here is a simple prayer you can pray:

> Father, thank You for sending Your only Son to die for my sins on the Cross, and for raising Him from the dead to give me a new spiritual life in Him. I give my life to You and promise to love and serve You all the days of my life. Amen.

By the time you take your last breath, you will have made your decision to pray this prayer or not, and you will either go to Heaven or to Hell. I hope that you will pray this prayer with all your heart and live for Jesus. There is no better way to live!

If you prayed that prayer, then you are going to dis-

cover that the earthly benefits are unbelievably wonderful. Jesus makes you complete and whole. Your life
now has purpose, and you will have joy in your heart,
even when the circumstances are hard. Wouldn't it be a
shame to not reap much in this world and also not reap
anything except punishment throughout all eternity?
And wouldn't it be a shame to have gained all kinds of
material wealth and happiness in this life, only to find
out that your pride kept you from receiving the greatest
blessing a human being can have: eternal life with God
through Jesus Christ?

Think about it. What do you have to lose by making this change in your life?

After we become a Christian, we enter the greatest
adventure imaginable. Reading the Bible opens our
eyes to so many truths and gives us so much under-
standing of life and how this world works, and the
Holy Spirit inside us is our great Teacher. We discover
how much God loves us and wants us to have the full
measure of His spiritual and natural blessings.

If you choose to ask for forgiveness for your sins

and accept Jesus as your Lord, your character will change. When you are spiritually joined with God you will exhibit a spirit of love, joy, peace, patience, kindness, goodness, faithfulness, gentleness, and self-control. You will have a yearning to please Him.

An example of what I'm talking about happened to a man who led a church not far from where June and I live. The building was small and needed to be expanded, and the Holy Spirit gave him a strong leading to ask the members of the church to give to a building fund. Furthermore, he felt that there were ten people who would contribute one thousand dollars. On the following Sunday, he told his congregation, "Let us sit in silence and allow God to speak to our hearts about what we should give." One by one people stood up and pledged to give a thousand dollars. Eventually, nine committed to this. One of them was a stranger to the group, but he said he felt like he should give. A little time passed, and the tenth person did not stand up. So they waited a little longer, silently praying for the Spirit to work.

Soon a member stood up and said he felt like he should give a thousand dollars *to the stranger*. The stranger stood up and said, "I'm a traveling evangelist, and God laid it on my heart to give to the fund. I told the Lord that all I had for my family to live on was this thousand dollars, and God said, 'I will give it back to you if you will do as I say.' I didn't realize it would be given back so soon!"

This is a great demonstration of how the Spirit of God will lead you and bless you if you just listen and obey. I desire to always have this kind of relationship with my God, and I am always asking Him to help me to stay close to Him, to be led by Him, and to allow His wisdom and strength to help me fulfill all He wants me to do.

What a limitless, awesome God we serve! We live on land He created, which has an ecosystem composed of billions of complex plant and animal life designed to perfection. I find it interesting that the scientific community, after studying different physical phenomena, again and again come to conclusions that are already stated as fact in the Bible. I have never thought the Bible to be at odds with science. After all, if God created everything, He knows how everything works and would at least hint at it in His Word. As the Creator, God would be the original and supreme scientist, engineer, medical expert, mathematician, psychologist, and so on.

As I see it, the problem with America is that too many of us have turned away from God and looked to the government to fix everything and give us all the answers to our problems. I hope and pray that Christians are realizing that they have no hope or answers in anything but God. I believe that if the church would come together, pray, work hard, treat everyone right, and trust God to move, things in this country and the world would change for the better.

In my 75 years, I've seen a lot of sunrises and learned a little most days. I've enjoyed a good measure of economic success, if you allow me to use my yardstick to measure my success. All this living and working to provide my family with what we needed and a little more just to add some spice to our lives has been rewarding. However, nothing compares with the love and joy imparted into me when I was born again. This born-again experience cannot be described with words. The only way you can know what I'm talking about is to surrender your heart and life to Jesus and experience the Holy Spirit coming to live inside you.

I don't have all the answers, even after all these years of reading and studying the Bible and being committed to follow Jesus and be like Him. But after all my years of living, and most of those years loving and serving Him, I know this for certain: We must love God with all of our hearts and put Him first in our lives, and then we must love and respect each other. That's how people become one and peace comes to a nation. And that's how peace will reign on the Earth — only through Jesus Christ our Savior, Lord, and King. Oh, how I love Jesus!

Epilogue

I took some time to share my life with you, and I hope you not only enjoyed it, but that it caused you to grow and learn in your own life. If you are a Christian, you know that there is nothing like the transformation that occurs within you when you are spiritually reborn and walk with Jesus. Now, I hope you are inspired to lead others to the Lord and will use this book to do that. That was the main reason I wrote it, because I want everyone I meet, as well as those I know and love, to experience the peace and confidence that can only be experienced by knowing God through Jesus Christ.

Thank you for allowing me to share a part of me with you. May the Lord bless you and may you have a long and happy life.

Article 1
Early Development of USA Roads

When the first automobiles found their way to the central plains states in America, there were only a few wagon and horse trails. They had no hard surface roads. These deficient trails passed through vast expanses of undeveloped land, there were no fuel or service stations, and weather conditions frequently changed the plans of the traveler. Great distances separated communities, and the roads were rough and often dusty, muddy, or washed out. There were no bridges, and many of the rivers and streams had fairly large deltas. Roads in this part of the country had a completely different set of problems to be solved.

The people who worked on these roads knew that well drained roadbeds held up better; therefore, the initial efforts were focused on raising the roadbed and providing drainage ditches along both sides. In the river deltas, this was more difficult because they were on almost level land, which was very hard to drain. The dirt removed to provide ditches was used to raise the level of the road.

Within one mile of my home, there is a natural deposit of clay and gravel mix at the right percentages to make a topping for gravel roads. No crushing is required because it is ready when dug up. I'm sure in most areas, these raw materials were not located so conveniently.

In the early days of building cars, the wheels and tires were narrow and tall. They may have built them that way because that's what they were used to looking at on horse-drawn buggies and wagons, or road conditions were such that these type of tires worked better. The top layers of soil were soft, and thin tires would sink down to firmer layers, allowing better traction. People in Oklahoma carried chains in their cars, which they called mud chains. These were the same as snow chains but were used more for mud than for snow. The autos of this era had a lot of ground clearance, which resulted in very deep ruts.

In later years the tires were changed to smaller diameters and greater widths. These cars had difficulty traveling on the same roads with ruts made by older, taller cars. They were built with less ground clearance. When they attempted to get through muddy strips of road, they would drag high center, making the dirt between the ruts very smooth. At times, the later model cars would get stuck in the center of the road. This would shut the road down, because there was only one set of ruts. There were places where you could pull over and wait for the oncoming car to make it through the bad spot, but if they were not able to get through, everyone waiting would get out of their cars to move the stuck car out of everyone's way.

Another obstacle they had to overcome was crossing streams. Whether large or small, the streams had to be crossed during dry and wet conditions. They searched for the best bank and stream bottom conditions, and most large rivers employed several variations of powered ferries. The ferry locations are still named for them, even though they were discontinued over fifty years ago. Here in Oklahoma we have Markham Ferry Lake, Greers Ferry Cove, and Taylor Ferry. The ferries were named after the family that ran them.

The road system in the US has been a work in progress for over one hundred years. The early developers of this system found it to be an arduous chore. They were a tough and determined group, with a need to carry goods and passengers. They were overcomers, and my hat is off to them.

Article 11
Development of the Automobile

Riding a horse or riding in a horse-drawn buggy, wagon, or stagecoach were reliable modes of travel. However, this method of travel was much too slow, and the endurance of the horses was too short. People needed a faster, more flexible way of moving goods and people around. The railroads were good, but they served a very small percentage of the land area.

The industrial entrepreneurs recognized the need to build a vehicle that would meet the needs of the American people. They had a few metals, wood, cotton, wool, rubber, tar, and leather as raw materials to build a vehicle. They had gasoline, oil, or coal for fuel and lubricants. They had some deep thinking, creative minds to figure out how to design the cars, and machinists and mechanics and other craftsmen to build them. The need for better transportation was the main driving force.

Some of the first autos lacked reliability. They had to be hand-cranked to start them. They did not have hydraulic brakes. They did not have any power-assisted steering. Most drivers were men, because it took strong bodies to crank, stop, and steer. Very few people had the knowledge to start and operate the cars in order to obtain a successful performance. Today, most operators would be just as unfamiliar. They would not know whether to advance or retard the spark or how to choke or prime the engine as needed. Modern cars do all of this and more automatically, but the users of early cars had to set these engine functions to get a good performance. Too often these control levers were set incorrectly, resulting in bad results or even disasters, such as broken limbs or destroyed engines and automobiles.

Early autos had simple, square bodies. Little attention was paid to the appearance. The glass consisted of flat pieces. The fenders, doors, hoods, and other small pieces were stamped out in metal presses. They were not able to stamp out the top with solid metal. This resulted in a large hole in the top of both coupes and sedans, which were filled with chicken wire and fibrous insulation, and then covered with a cotton cloth coated with a tar-like substance. These tops soon leaked, destroying the framing materials of the body.

The engines were difficult to cool. The craftsmen were not able to construct efficient radiators out of very thin materials that would transfer the heat out of the coolant, like we have today. Even if they had the ability and the materials, the rough roads and poor suspension would probably have destroyed the delicate radiators anyway.

These first cars had kerosene lights on them. When I was young, an old man said that when he was a boy he would get out and run behind the car as it was slowly going up a hill and light the taillights with a match. I don't believe this type of lighting would enable you to see the road, but it would allow you to be seen by other drivers. The vehicle soon had an electrical system, which included lights, instrumentation, generator, batteries, and starter.

Our first car tires were made out of natural rubber over woven cotton cords. They were easy to destroy and had to be lined with an inner tube to hold the air inside. All drivers carried jacks, lug wrenches, patching material, and a hand pump. You would witness a lot of tire repair along the roads.

When they were dry, the dirt roads would break down into dust, which would swirl up and around and get into the passenger compartment. You would have to breath it. When the same roads were wet, you could hear the mud hitting the underside of the vehicle. When either of these conditions existed, it was apparent that we needed good seals to keep contaminants out and lubricants in all moving joints. Anything less than perfect made the life of the equipment short.

These automobiles did not last as long as they do today. The manufacturers addressed these issues with some degree of success. When reliability levels became acceptable, the auto manufacturers turned some of their attention to the comfort of the people inside the cars. They began to put heaters in them and devised ways to cool people by diverting outside air onto the feet of passengers. Tilt-out windshields and winged side windows were added for upper body cooling. They built better suspension for smoother rides, and more comfortable seats were installed in roomier interiors.

In the late 1920s the automobile was mass-produced, enabling it to be sold at prices that allowed a workingman to have and use the automobile for his family. It was no longer thought of as a luxury. The car became a necessity.

Article 111
Impact of the Depression on the Automobile Industry

In 1929, the stock market crashed. Many people lost their jobs. Others who kept their jobs experienced excessive salary cuts. Businesses closed. Banks went broke. Rich people saw their wealth evaporate. Their stocks were worth nothing. The closing of the banks made them lose all their money. All this economic distress caused the buying public to think differently. The market for selling automobiles changed drastically, as did other markets selling consumable products.

People who had the money to buy were not eager to part with it. The auto industry had to adapt to these new conditions. One thing became clear to all of the manufacturers: They were going to have to offer more to the buyer than they had in years past. In 1932, they made more changes to improve the appearance than they had in previous years, but there were even more noticeable and numerous changes in 1933.

All manufacturers improved the outward appearance of the full line of body styles. They added more chrome to V-shaped grilles. They had beautiful headlights, taillights, bumpers, external trumpet horns, hood doors, and side-mounted spares. Some of these features were on earlier models, but on 1933 models it was common to see all of them. Bringing fenders down in front and adding vertical skirts behind the front wheels covered suspension parts, which were not attractive. They put the tires in the fender wells. Even with all this attention focused on eye appeal, many of the companies only sold a few hundred automobiles in each body style.

The year 1933 is my favorite transitional year. More body improvements were made during that year than any other. The value of a vehicle is definitely impacted by the scarcity of it. During these extremely low production years, other circumstances reduced these numbers even further. For instance, in the 1930s cars were mostly driven on bad roads, so their life was short.

Then, near the end of the life of these cars, the US needed steel for armor to use in World War II. The government asked citizens to bring in their cars and other metal equipment to be crushed for this need. Many old cars were lost to the war effort, so the survivors are real treasures.